ADVANCE PRAISE

"Kelly Siegel's story of addiction and excess is a very telling reminder that all of us have some level of hurt and pain in our lives. No one ever has the perfect blueprint for life. But we humans are amazing creatures. To compensate for fear, doubts, and pain, we can put on facades that show others that we have the most energy, joy, and fulfillment.

"That's why I'm so happy that Siegel had his 'aha' moment on the beach. Not all those dealing with addiction have what it takes to make a successful recovery, but Siegel is making the most of his second chance.

"Many of the ten values that guide Kelly's life are those that guide mine and should guide yours too. But isn't it amazing that it's hard to follow a common-sense blueprint even when the ideas are so easy to grasp? While it's one thing to make the recovery, it's another thing to teach others not to follow your path. I love Kelly's mission on giving back. That's how we all get better (AGB) all day, everyday. Take the time to read this, and you will benefit."

—JAYSON WALLER, CEO

"In his memoir, Kelly Siegel transparently opens up about his very personal journey through scarcity, struggle, abuse, addiction, and self destruction. He unselfishly shares his own daily practices, disciplines, and fail-proof action items, with the intent to help, guide, and mentor his readers toward self discovery, healing, and ultimately living a life of true self worth and abundance. A must-read for anyone looking for an inspirational, feel-good true story about overcoming the odds and triumphantly 'winning' at the game of life."

—KRISTEN CULLEN, FOUNDER, MENTOR, COACH, BRAND STRATEGIST

"Kelly's journey reminds us that clear thinking is about courage instead of intelligence. That living your best life begins with remembering your life. Sometimes that means leaving the party."

—RICK HARBER, FOUNDER & CEO

"When I first met Kelly, I quickly realized two things. First, he was very determined, disciplined, and committed; I knew this by observing his training in the gym. Yes, he is in outstanding shape, he is consistent. Second, I felt genuine and authentic kindness coming from his words. Frequently, we meet people, and it feels like we were bitten by a vampire, drained. With Kelly, you feel inspired and motivated to kick ass and make your goals happen today!

"I look forward to applying his lessons and taking life to the next level!"

—JEFF JACOBS, INTERNET STRATEGIST

HARDER THAN LIFE

HARDER THAN LIFE

OVERCOMING POVERTY, ADDICTION, AND VIOLENCE

KELLY SIEGEL

HARDER THAN LIFE
Overcoming Poverty, Addiction, and Violence

FIRST EDITION

ISBN   978-1-5445-3912-6 *Hardcover*
         978-1-5445-3913-3 *Paperback*
         978-1-5445-3978-2 *Ebook*

To my sister Lesia, who saved me from many savage beatings. I would not be here today without your courage to stand up to our mother and stepfather. You are the strong one.

To my daughter Arianna, you are my Why. Darlin', the cycle stops with us. I love you dearly.

To anyone going through tough times. You are not alone, and you are Harder than Life.

CONTENTS

INTRODUCTION

As the sun came up on New Year's Day 2007, I was sitting on the crescent-shaped beach of Haad Rin in Thailand, doing shots with Liam Neeson. People were passed out in the sand all around us. I had no idea where my buddies were.

Stumbling back to my hotel, a brutal hangover made it near impossible to piece together the night that started coming back to me in flashes. I'd taken the insane journey to Koh Phangan with ten friends to attend Haad Rin's infamous Full Moon Party, which coincided closely with New Year's Eve.

One of my last completely lucid memories was having dinner at a Mexican restaurant and popping ecstasy. It was so strong that it hit me within three minutes, and everything after that had been one giant blur of excess. If it sounds like the movie *The Hangover Part II*, you're not wrong.

When we got to the beach, about twenty thousand people were already partying. Full Moon Party is an all-night banger with bars stretching the entire length of the beach, each blasting a different genre of music—hip hop, country, rock, you name it. Maybe because I was high on ecstasy, maybe because there were a gazillion people, I lost my buddies a few hours into getting there. I kept drinking on my own.

At 2:00 a.m., the party was still going, and the heat and humidity had barely let up. I was hot and tired and completely wasted, so I decided to sit down at a booth and order a smoothie to cool down. It wasn't until I started hallucinating that I noticed the booth was shaped like a giant mushroom.

Soon, the paranoia set in.

Here I was, drunk, high, and hallucinating, alone in a foreign country plunged into chaos by a military coup and civil unrest. A few days later, officials would shut down the city, barricade our hotel, and bomb the very place that was currently packed with thousands of people.

I thought I was going to die, and I didn't even care. But a tiny part of me knew this was it. I couldn't take it anymore. And neither could my liver. I had been angry for so long that being reckless and excessive felt like a relief, even if only a temporary one. But as I looked around bleary-eyed at people gearing up for the after-party, I just wanted to go home.

I took the next flight to the US. I'd blown $20,000 on a vacation I spent largely too intoxicated to enjoy; gone to a brothel with a prominent (married) news anchor who would later run for Senate; partied with wealthy, successful movers and shakers;

and ended it all on a beach, pounding shots with a famous actor. Around thousands of people, I only felt crushing loneliness.

I didn't know exactly what I wanted, but I knew this wasn't it.

I want to tell you that I got my shit together after this, but I didn't. My daughter Arianna was born two years later, in early 2009. It still took me almost a decade to realize that my love for her was the ultimate *Why* that would eventually help me quit using.

We all have demons; some of us just have a few more than average (raises hand). Whether yours are addictions to alcohol, drugs, sex, gambling, or work, it doesn't matter. Throw in some childhood trauma, abuse, neglect, or poverty, and you have a volatile combo that will eventually catch up with you.

One of the reasons I didn't quit drinking earlier is because I truly believed I did my best work hungover. People loved drunk Kelly, both personally and professionally. Hell, many of my clients were my drinking buddies and vice versa. I was wild and reckless and drank everyone under the table, then got up at 5:00 a.m. to lift and put in a full day at work. It felt like a badge of honor, like proving my toughness. It got to the point where my friends coined the term "getting siegeled" for partying their asses off. Someone would pass out on my boat, in my car, or at my house, and I'd post a picture of their drunk ass on social media saying they got *siegeled*.

My father and grandfather's last name *Siegel* had come to mean excess, addiction, and material success. My life felt hollow. I was lonely. I wanted my life and my name to mean something bigger.

What my friends didn't know, and what I kept even from myself most of the time was that I used alcohol as a crutch. My identity as the fun drinking buddy and savvy businessman with the gregarious personality and imposing physical stature was all a mask. Nobody knew why I'd spent so much time at the gym getting huge. Nobody knew what was under the big smile. I constantly pursued the next deal, the next woman, the next material status symbol. I blew all my money on vacations, cars, boats, fancy dinners, designer clothes, and jewelry because I wanted to wash off the stink of poverty and because I thought it would make me happy.

You already know what I'll say next: today, I've got more than enough money and, still, I sometimes worry about it. A comfortable life and material luxuries are nice, but they did not make me happy. It's cliché but true.

I knew part of finding happiness and meaning was dealing with the anger, grief, and resentment left over from my childhood. I knew I had to face those demons once and for all. Until then, I knew my life would continue on as it was: I was an involved dad but never fully present as a drunk. I was successful in my business but didn't know how to take it to the next level. I was constantly involved with different women but rarely experienced a genuine connection. I'd built my physical strength but neglected my emotional and mental health.

I had no tools, no experience, and very few role models.

I grew up dirt poor near 8 Mile in Detroit and went to high school with Eminem. If you've seen his movie *8 Mile*, you have a pretty good idea of what my life was like (minus the rap star ambitions). I lived in a small, cramped home in South Warren, a neighborhood riddled with poverty, drugs, and violence. My mom, dad, and stepdad were alcoholics and drug addicts.

I got my first job at twelve—not to buy comic books and video games but food. I've been in more street fights than I can count because my friends were my family, and we had to have each other's backs. Most of these childhood friends are now dead or in prison. I've had knives and guns drawn on me, been arrested for selling cocaine, and gone to jail. I even made it to college against all odds, only to be kicked out. I've had more drinks and taken more drugs than anyone else I know. Worst of all, the people who were supposed to love and care for me tried to kill me more than once.

In other words, I shouldn't be here today—but I am.

In this book, I'll tell you my story and share the ten values that guide my personal and professional life: self-awareness, honesty and integrity, communication, family, loyalty, growth, health, tenacity, results, and legacy.

None of these concepts are new. I don't have a fucking magic pill—and if I did, you can be sure I would've downed the entire bottle of it, with a vodka chaser to boot. This book isn't a one-size-fits-all self-help book that lays out five easy steps to overnight success. This is my story of how I worked my ass off to build a life I love.

Maybe you can relate to having a lot of personal and professional success, loads of "friends," and a lucrative business or career—or at least the appearance of that from the outside looking in. Perhaps you, too, are always looking over your shoulder despite your success, or know there's a looming issue in your life that you haven't yet dealt with. Or maybe you just know that things could be better, that you could be happier. I hope sharing my experience will inspire you to take action in your own life.

In this book, you'll find no-bullshit mentorship and guidance for creating a personal framework for growth and development in your life. If you're serious about getting your shit together, reach out directly (check the back of the book for my personal contact info). I'm committed to paying it forward and giving others what I wish I'd had when I needed it most.

This book isn't just another boring dime-a-dozen, politically correct rags-to-riches story in the self-help section. My approach to personal growth and self-development is both empathetic and brutally honest. Eventually, we all have to decide whether we're ready to embrace the suck to get what we want...or not.

In each chapter and for each value, I'll share some outrageous stories, painful truths, practical life wisdom, and business advice that has worked for me. Most importantly, I'll give you tools, activities, and resources to implement into your daily life. Take what you like and leave the rest.

Talk is cheap, and while I devour books all day, it's continually putting what I learn into action that is helping me create the life I want. I'll be the friend who commiserates with you when you're having a hard time (for about twenty minutes), and then I'll kick your ass to the gym and problem solve with you on how to get you healthy, fix your business, and find a therapist who will help you address your demons.

As you read this book, I want you to think of one positive change you can commit to for ninety days.

Every book I read, every podcast I listen to, and every expert I learn from has given me a piece of the puzzle at the right time. I hope you'll find that one puzzle piece you need most right now in these pages.

Life is hard, but I'm harder. If you're still reading, you've got it in you, too.

The life you want is waiting for you.

CHAPTER ONE

SELF-AWARENESS

My first job was dumping out my stepdad's piss jar every day. He was addicted to alcohol and pills, and so was my mom. Their relationship was volatile, which often led to confrontations and violent fights. When I was eight years old, he started locking himself in the bedroom to get away from her. He wouldn't even come out to use the bathroom, and relieved himself into a jar instead. It was my responsibility to empty that jar every day. This first job came with shitty pay (zero dollars) and a beating, if I forgot. Sometimes, when my stepdad was feeling especially petty and cruel, he dumped the jar all over my bed if he deemed I didn't take care of it quickly enough.

I felt worthless when my stepdad treated me this way. It was disgusting and embarrassing, and there was nothing I could do about it. He was tall, heavy, violent, and unpredictable, and he seemed like a giant to me. The helplessness I felt made me angry. Scrawny little me swore I would grow huge and get out of there as soon as possible—but not without punching my stepdad in the face on my way out the door.

It didn't quite happen that way, but eventually, I got out. In some twisted way, the piss jar taught me to do whatever it took. Of course, what my stepdad did was horrible, and no child deserves to be treated that way. And yet, it also helped me realize then that no matter what anyone else does to me, they will not break me. Those difficult early experiences made me who I am today. I didn't know it at the time, but the self-awareness that who I was and who I would become was not dependent on anyone else, saved my life.

Before self-awareness transformed my life, I tried absolutely everything to run away from myself and the demons of my past. I saw and experienced a lot of addiction, poverty, anger, and violence growing up.

I lived with my mom, stepdad, and sister in a small house off of 8 Mile in Warren, a suburb of Detroit. My mom and dad had a brief relationship, but they never lived together. My sister had a different dad, but since she was nine years older than me, by the time I came along, he was already out of the picture. The stepdad whose house we both grew up in had met our mom at a bar and invited her to live with him. Apparently, she took him up on that offer one day and showed up at his doorstep—she'd just failed to mention our existence. It was not an ideal way to start a blended family. My mom, dad, and stepdad were all alcoholics, and my dad became a heroin addict during my early teen years.

I had the hunger and drive to get out of there and succeed, but I lacked good coping mechanisms for dealing with the pain and anger. Instead, I turned to alcohol and drugs, like my parents.

This chapter is about the crutches and masks I used to numb

myself, hide, and escape reality. I'll tell you how I quit drinking, and dispel the myths of rock bottom and powerlessness over our demons. I'll share with you what I believe is the root cause of reaching for any crutch, and what I do to protect and maintain my newfound self-awareness.

Before I stopped drinking in 2019, my life looked incredible from the outside. My business was growing. I was in a relationship with a woman I loved. I co-parented my daughter with my ex-wife. I had plenty of material success and was surrounded by people who loved me, and who I loved.

Life was good, but I was never fully happy, never content. I was always mad, a low level of frustration simmering just under the surface. The smallest thing was enough to trigger me to lose my cool. I'd become dismissive, insensitive, and even mean. Usually, that behavior led me to drink more to numb those feelings.

People talk about rock bottom all the time, but the truth is, I never reached it. I don't even know if I was a real alcoholic. But I do know that I was drunk all the time. I was a smart drunk, a high-functioning drunk, a successful drunk, but a drunk nonetheless. I just got so damn tired of the same cycle.

Alcohol was an easy way to distract and escape the anger, sadness, and loneliness that were always present. Whether you call it a mask or a crutch, it kept me from unpacking why I was still so unhappy and what was missing in my life. For the longest time, I didn't want to explore what was going on.

When I finally did, it wasn't the result of a dramatic incident. I didn't lose my company. I didn't run out of money. I didn't end up in jail. I didn't lose all the people I loved. There was no *one* thing.

ARE YOU STILL WAITING TO HIT ROCK BOTTOM? DON'T.

The idea that we have to hit rock bottom to start making changes is bullshit.

I never hit rock bottom, but I could see it coming. The writing was on the wall, and I saw people all around me destroy their lives because of alcohol and substance abuse. My stepdad got nine DUIs and crashed his car before finally quitting. Most of my childhood friends ended up dead or in jail due to alcohol and drug overdoses or accidents. I was arrested and went to jail for selling cocaine. I knew I was one bad decision away from ruining my life permanently and losing everything: my daughter, my business, and maybe my life. I never hit rock bottom, but I thought about it constantly.

For me, it was enough to realize that when I drank, I turned into someone I didn't like. I wasn't my best self anymore. I didn't want to be angry, frustrated, and miserable. I didn't want to wake up in the morning hungover, and with a hazy recollection of dumb shit I said that I would have to apologize for. I was pissing away money on material things that meant nothing to me, and partying with people who weren't true friends. I wanted to take that money and do more worthwhile things with it— save it, invest it into my business, build a house, and donate to charitable causes. I was tired of having a chip on my shoulder. I realized my anger often made me feel stuck and like a victim. I acted like the whole world was against me, so I could never hold any space for good things to come into my life.

My fiancée and I had plans for New Year's 2018/19 in Key West, but she never showed up. We'd gotten into a fight over her repeatedly cheating on me, and she'd run off to hook up with yet another dude, so I broke it off. It had been a toxic cycle of on-again-off-again that I couldn't seem to escape. Later I'd find out that she was partying in Fort Lauderdale with a bunch of my friends, while I was getting drunk in Key West on my own. If that sounds fucking sad, it was. I thought I didn't deserve better. I was embarrassed and lonely and wondering why things weren't working out. After having too many meaningless flings, I was done being a drunk whore, and I didn't want to date other drunk whores anymore. I loved my fiancée, although our relationship was rocky. I was hurt by her repeated cheating, but I wanted to work out our issues together. I had a vague sense that alcohol could be exacerbating our problems, and I wanted to give it a fair shot. I decided to quit drinking that night.

As I dragged my ass from bar to bar on Duval Street, a surly prick of a bar owner poured me a gigantic scotch with a rock ball. I kept drinking scotch and whiskey until, at 2:00 a.m., I decided I was done. Not just for the day—but *done*. I left my last drink sitting on the bar and stumbled back to my empty hotel room to pass out. I stayed in the room most of New Year's Day with a horrible hangover, shaking, and unable to eat. I used to say, *Hey, it's only a hangover if you stop drinking.* This time, I experienced the full consequences of poisoning my body with alcohol.

The shaking got worse on day two, and by day three, when I had to fly home for a funeral, my anxiety was through the roof. I hate flying any time, but with the shakes, it was a whole new level of misery. By day four, the withdrawals and anxiety had me trembling and crying uncontrollably in the pew at my friend's father's funeral. I was so embarrassed that I snuck out. Day five I spent crying. Yes, pretty much the entire day. I called one of my best friends, Anthony, who told me I was a good person who'd made some bad choices. He told me he loved me and was there for me, and I burst into tears again.

I was in a bad way, reeling from physical withdrawals and feeling like the world was crumbling around me. I sat down in my kitchen, which was still stocked with alcohol, and pulled out the gun I always carry. I looked at the bottles of booze and my gun. In that moment of deep desperation, I knew I didn't want to reach for either. Neither one of them was an option or a solution to my problems. I knew then that I believed in myself and would see myself through.

The phone rang, and it was another close friend of mine, Jesse, checking on me. When he heard how terrible I was doing, he came over. Jesse dragged me to the gym, where I put in a half-ass workout. Then he took me home and informed me that he was staying over. We cooked dinner together and were sitting down for a meal when my daughter came home. He gave me true friendship, support, and a semblance of normalcy on one of my darkest days.

I continued to feel like absolute dog shit for days but didn't see a doctor. I got myself into that mess, and I wanted to get myself out. I don't recommend this approach. It just shows that I always felt I had to do it all on my own without help and support from anyone else. I quit drinking cold turkey, but I'm not saying anyone else should do it like that. I chose this path because I'm used to doing everything on my own. I like taking the hard path because that's how I learn the quickest. That's not a badge of honor. It's just self-awareness based on my personality and life experience.

There are dangers to quitting cold turkey because you'll experience intense physical and emotional withdrawals that should be supervised by a medical professional. If you want to go to a group or rehab, do it. It doesn't matter how; what matters is that you find the approach that works for you. I considered rehab and spoke with several members of Alcoholics Anonymous to decide what would work best for me. The first step of AA is: "We admitted we were powerless over alcohol—that our lives had become unmanageable." I hate everything about that. You don't tell me I'm powerless, and you don't tell me that I can't do something. That's never going to work for me. I never felt powerless over alcohol. I didn't quit sooner because I didn't *want* to, not because I couldn't. I understand this isn't popular to say, but it's true for me. I felt powerless for so much of my childhood that I focused my adulthood on reclaiming my power. A program centered around powerlessness simply would not work for me. I knew that much. For some people, that is exactly what helps them and attracts them to AA, and that's wonderful. I have some friends who swear by AA and credit decades of sobriety to it.

It all comes down to self-awareness and knowing who you are and what will work for you. For me, it was quitting cold turkey while also working with a therapist. I gravitate more toward an approach that puts me in control and empowers me to determine my relationship with alcohol. I've found Annie Grace's book *This Naked Mind* incredibly helpful in looking honestly at what fueled my need to drink. For me, it was the ever-present feeling of not being good enough.

I got off social media and stopped hanging out with my drinking buddies. I had only told a few people that I quit—my aunt and uncle, and a couple of close friends. People were skeptical, and I didn't want anyone's opinions and attitudes to influence me. About halfway through January, I started feeling better. I ran into my ex-fiancée at a big charity event. I hadn't seen her since our breakup right before New Year's. She was already drunk and acting stupid, and I was finally starting to feel alive. I realized in that moment the difficult two weeks leading up to the event had been worth it. I needed to keep going on the path of sobriety. Of course, that didn't mean I made only good decisions from that moment forward. That night I didn't know that I would take her back yet again, only to have her cheat, disappear, and come running back. As we all know, the definition of insanity is doing the same thing over and over again and expecting a different result. By that definition, I was definitely insane.

Quitting cold turkey doesn't mean it was easy. The thing nobody tells you is that quitting drinking isn't the hardest part of giving up alcohol. The hardest part is dealing with the shit that made you drink in the first place while sober. Being fully sober as four decades of trauma and pain crashed down around me was hell. If I'd known how hard my first year of sobriety would be, I would not have quit. I spent many nights curled up in a 220-pound ball on my couch, sobbing uncontrollably. I could've had a drink, or distracted myself—but I didn't. I'm still not sure how I got through, except that no matter how lonely I was, or how terrible I felt, at least I was alive and truly experiencing my emotions.

While the quitting worked, the relationship did not. A little over a year into my sobriety, we broke up for good right before

COVID lockdowns in March 2020. I couldn't do it any longer. I realized that I couldn't force anyone to change. I could only be responsible for myself. I no longer wanted to live in a haze of alcohol and drugs. I wanted a real relationship, authentic connection, and genuine loyalty. I wanted to build a life with someone. The relationship didn't work out for multiple reasons, but one of them was that I quit, and she didn't. That's when I realized that while I might have stopped drinking for her, she wouldn't be my reason for staying sober. I had gotten a taste of what it felt like to be truly present in my life, to be self-aware for the first time, not dulled by any substances. I had gained clarity on what I wanted and who I wanted to be. I would not give that up. Once I gained a level of self-awareness, it was much harder to be around people who were still escaping from reality on a regular basis.

We went our separate ways and years later, I still don't have the relationship I want. It sucks, and at the same time, it helped me realize that I'm not doing this to get something. Being alone, sober, and self-aware is still better than being drunk and in a toxic relationship. This journey of self-awareness, presence, and personal growth is meaningful for its own sake.

EMOTION SUPPRESSION IS THE ROOT CAUSE

If I'd known about the tidal wave of overwhelming emotions that would crash over me once I threw my crutch away, I would have never stopped drinking. But if I didn't suppress these emotions to begin with, I never would have started drinking in the first place. If I'd gotten help or therapy of any kind as a kid, teenager, or college student, maybe I could have been spared decades of drinking to numb the pain. But there was nobody to pull me aside and tell me, hey, you gotta deal with this trauma. Your mom and stepdad tried to kill you. You had no food to eat. You were abandoned. These thoughts of being unlovable, unworthy, and never good enough are false. These feelings of anger and depression make perfect sense, given your background of poverty, violence, and addiction. Your coping mechanisms served you well in helping you to survive, but they will hurt you long-term. Your feelings must be processed. They won't go away by you trying to escape from them or numb them with substances, work, women, and material success.

I wish someone had said this to me when I was younger, so I'm saying it to you now: *suppressing your emotions will wreak havoc on your life.* You can look successful on the outside when you follow that script, but you will not feel peace or joy on the inside. Especially as men, all we've ever heard from our dads and grandpas, coaches and bosses, brothers and friends is some variation of: Suck it up. Don't be a pussy. Get over it. Quit crying, or I'll give you something to cry about.

Enough with that bullshit. You can be a hardass motherfucker with feelings. Being vulnerable is the new cool. It takes courage to deal with pain, rather than just ignoring it. It takes strength to be vulnerable and honest, instead of pretending that nothing and no one matters to you. You can only be that fucking buffalo running into the storm if your strength and confidence come from within.

WHAT ARE YOU TRYING TO MASK?

You must deal with the issues and feelings under the surface that make you want to use a crutch in the first place. Throwing my crutch away was only the beginning. The harder, more important work is figuring out why I started using that crutch in the first place. What was I trying to escape from? What feelings did I need to numb? What temporary benefits did I get from drinking?

My parents abandoned me for alcohol and drugs, and then I chose alcohol and drugs as a source of comfort.

You must fill that empty space with something good for you that will support your self-awareness and presence in a healthy way. Otherwise, you'll never be truly free and deeply present in your life.

For me, the biggest crutches were alcohol, drugs, and chasing women and material success, but anything can keep you numb and distracted from your real life. Doesn't even matter if it's legal or illegal. There are lots of legal crutches that can totally fuck up your life, like scrolling Instagram for hours or gambling all your money away. Chances are you have a pretty good idea of what your crutch is. It's that behavior, substance, or coping skill you feel protective of or even defensive about, the one that requires a lot of justifications and explanations. You're probably thinking about it right now!

You can't just eliminate this massive part of your life without expecting something else to fill its place. If you leave a vacuum, it will be flooded. We all know these people. They quit drinking and consider themselves sober, but they still smoke pot or take mushrooms. Just because you call something "medicine" doesn't mean it's not doing exactly the same thing the alcohol was. Just because it's a plant doesn't mean you're less likely to use it as an escape.

My uncle still drinks, but he's complained loudly and frequently that because of me, he must now ask himself, "What am I trying to mask?" whenever he wants to drink. Everyone is on their own path and makes decisions that feel right for them, but I'm glad he's starting to question his motives. Maybe you will, too.

IT TAKES A VILLAGE

I've been on my own, fighting for survival since I was a little boy, so reaching out for help and accepting kindness from others is still extremely uncomfortable for me. However, I know that most problems aren't created alone, and they're not solved alone. It's tough to implement in practice because my default is to feel responsible, take charge of everything, and feel like I can't ask for or rely on the help of others. I'm slowly learning that surrounding myself with good, honest, supportive people helps me be more self-aware.

I may have lost drinking buddies when I got sober, but I've gained true friends who tell it like it is, even if I don't want to hear it. These friends have checked on me, taken me out to dinner and the gym, talked me through hard days, and encouraged me. I worried about reaching out to therapists and coaches because I didn't think it was okay for me to ask for support, but they've helped me make sense of my past and psyche and pushed me to become more self-aware. I may have lost business partners, employees, and clients in the process, but I've attracted others who are more closely aligned with my company's vision and share the appreciation for personal and professional progress. I have had to end some unhealthy relationships with women (including ending an engagement), but disentangling myself from these toxic dynamics has allowed me to see myself and my coping mechanisms more clearly. I cut off contact or minimized interactions with some family members who don't support my sobriety or personal growth. In return, I have forged deeper, more meaningful relationships with my family members who are open to change.

People who reach out to me about quitting drinking often tell me that they're scared of losing people in their lives. I don't tell them it won't happen—because it will. But consider this: Aren't you already lonely now? Don't you already have the sneaking suspicion that beyond drinking or doing drugs or partying, those relationships don't hold much substance? Aren't you a tiny bit curious about the level of self-awareness you might gain, and the new relationships you might attract into your life?

The most miserable sober day is still better than the best day I ever had as a drunk. I truly experience my life now. I'm present. I'm self-aware. And this self-awareness is the foundation for living an honest life with integrity.

CHAPTER TWO

HONESTY & INTEGRITY

I got a paper route at twelve—because I was hungry.

Between the ages of eight and twelve, when my mom and step-dad descended deeper into their alcohol and drug addictions, I was on my own, always scared, always hungry. As a twelve-year-old kid, after enduring years of violence and neglect, I knew I had to take care of myself to survive. Nobody was coming to save me.

I lied and said I was thirteen so I could start a paper route. I had to lie because the more important truth was that I had to make money so I could eat. It turned out that the paper route I was assigned to had been neglected and low on subscribers, so the first thing I did was knock on every door along the route and promise I would deliver their paper on time, every time, rain or shine. I tripled the subscriber base. Yes, I had to lie to get the job, but I was 100 percent honest with my customers. I came through for them every single day because I was driven to eat and to survive.

To this day, money means survival and food to me, although I haven't had an empty belly for a very long time.

In this chapter, we'll discuss how to live a life with integrity, side-stepping the common pitfalls of claiming capital T truth, not walking the talk, and cherry-picking the areas of life we want to live truthfully.

THE PROBLEM WITH CAPITAL T TRUTH

None of us have the *Truth*, but we act like we do. While I 100 percent believe in being honest, I'm very careful when it comes to throwing around the word *truth*. What each of us believe to be "the truth" actually are perspectives, opinions, and attitudes. It's essential to ensure our ideas are well-researched and informed, based on the most comprehensive and accurate facts we can access. But even then, we cannot help looking at everything and everyone through our specific lens, shaped by our background, personality, DNA, life experience, and beliefs.

I try to keep this in mind when disagreeing with anyone. Sometimes we may disagree on the facts, but more often, we're actually disagreeing over our interpretations of these facts. Instead of calling someone a liar, I instead try to listen more to understand why they see a situation differently than I do. The quickest way to shut down a discussion is to pretend there's only one way to look at a set of facts. That's how we collectively wound up in today's incredibly divisive political climate. We must withhold judgment as much as we can, listen more, talk less, and find common ground to have honest, productive conversations.

HALF-ASSING HONESTY

My stepdad is pretty much the biggest dick I have ever met. But he was as honest as the day was long. He was a manual laborer who did very well for himself, considering he was a high school dropout. I believe that, at least partially, it was because he could be relied upon to follow through on what he said. When it came to work, he did the right thing. He was always on time, never missed work because he was hungover, and had absolute integrity in his work ethic. It's too bad that honesty and integrity at work didn't translate to our home life. When I confronted him about the piss jar after I'd moved out, he denied it ever happened. I understand we all like to believe we're one of the good guys, so it's natural to block out painful or shameful memories. But, come on! Until you're honest in every aspect of your life, you're not truly honest.

Although I wasn't violent and cruel like my mom or stepdad, I rationalized and justified my own bullshit all the time when I was still drinking: I was a functioning drunk, so it wasn't a real problem. I never drank and drove, so I could call myself responsible. I never physically hurt anyone, so I conveniently forgot the other shitty things I said and did to hurt people. I had very few people in my life who held me accountable for my behavior, which made it harder to realize how much I was hurting myself and others. I'm not blaming people for not speaking up because I didn't listen to the few who did, like my therapist. All I'm saying is that sobriety was a rude awakening: I looked at my past behavior honestly for the first time and realized how much damage I had caused to people I love.

BE IMPECCABLE WITH YOUR WORD

It drives me nuts when I ask my daughter Ari to give her dog food and water every day, and she does it maybe 25 percent of the time. Yes, she's a teenager and has other things on her mind, but I believe it's important to teach my kid that if you say you're going to do something, do it. Everyone is forgetful sometimes, or has legitimate reasons for not following through on their commitments once in a while. But when it becomes a pattern, that's where I draw the line. That's no longer a forgetfulness issue but an integrity issue. I'm impeccable with my word, and I expect others to do the same. Yes, even my 13-year-old.

Integrity means that a person's actions align with their words. I have learned that I need to be very careful with my promises because I'll have to hold myself to them. I've often told Ari I'm sorry she's my kid because my standards are high, and I expect a lot from her. I try to teach by example, rather than lecture, so she knows that I follow through on whatever I tell her I will do and make it happen.

During those decades when I was wrestling with my demons, I rarely lied about my issues. I took responsibility when I fucked up. Unfortunately, that sometimes made me feel like being honest about my shortcomings was all I needed to do. I despised lying and liars, so I figured I could be an honest drunk and that alone would fix the problems. That didn't work out very well. Eventually, I realized that being honest was only the first step to taking control of my life. I had to follow it up with action.

IF YOU HAVE TO SAY YOU ARE SOMETHING, YOU PROBABLY AREN'T

I don't have to tell anyone that I work out; it's obvious. Similarly, if I had to tell anyone that I'm honest, it would mean I'm doing too much convincing and not enough modeling by example. I view lying in the same way I view taking a drink: if I slip once, it's easier to slip again. Why even open the door? Of course, it's not easy, but nothing worthwhile in life is. Easy choices, hard life. Hard choices, easy life.

Being honest requires being vulnerable, and that's uncomfortable and risky. Some people won't respond well to honesty or vulnerability, and that may be hurtful to you. However, the right people will appreciate your honesty. It's a natural selection process. The people who aren't ready to be real will run the other way. Good! Let them run. Lean into the discomfort of being honest and see what it can teach you. Remember you'll have to meet that same standard. Is your ego trying to protect you from being truly honest with yourself? Is your fear of rejection and abandonment getting in your way of setting and holding healthy boundaries? Books and therapy are your friends. Meditation and mindfulness, self-compassion, and acceptance all help buffer the discomfort of vulnerability and honesty.

INTEGRITY = REFUSING TO CHEAT MYSELF OR OTHERS

What is the point of cheating at golf? If I cheat, I'll know I didn't really win. If I take a shortcut and nobody knows, I still have to look at myself in the mirror. I'll know, and that's worse than the judgment of anyone else. How you do anything is how you do everything. That's why I'm suspicious of people who are shady in any aspect of their personal or professional lives. A lack of honesty and integrity in one thing bleeds into everything.

A few years ago, we sold a service to our customers that we had to acquire for our company National Technology Management (NTM) first. Then we started getting that service for free, and one of my employees asked if that meant we should stop charging our customers for it. I only had to point toward the sign with our company values including honesty and integrity, and he answered the question himself. You can find all of NTM's core values in Appendix A.

Honesty may be a hindrance to a bigger bottom line in the short term, but nothing beats the feeling of doing right by myself, my work family, and our customers. I have screwed myself out of deals because I have given prospective clients the bad news about how much it would realistically cost and how much time it would take to implement our best practices. I'd close more deals if I was willing to twist reality a bit, but I'm not looking for a quick buck. I want people to trust me and, by extension, my company, which means that showing integrity in everything we do is paramount.

YOU'RE NOT FOR SALE—DON'T SACRIFICE YOUR INTEGRITY

We've all sacrificed our integrity at some point. A couple of years ago, I onboarded a customer who wanted to save money, and went against my standards and better judgment to please them. I deviated from NTM's best practices to keep this customer happy instead of cutting them loose and wishing them well with another company. Their legacy firewall and wireless connection, which I didn't replace to save them money, went bad and created a security gap. I went against my professional integrity and paid for it.

But as the saying goes, losers assign blame, winners fix problems. I made the decision, so I fixed the issue when it arose. It cost more money and time than requiring the customer to do it right in the first place. It was an expensive but necessary reminder that, in the end, it always costs me to deviate from my standards.

REWARDING HONESTY WITH MY WORK FAMILY

Making mistakes is inevitable. Lying about them is not. Tell me the truth, and I've got your back. Always. Lie to me and find yourself in a shit storm of epic proportions. Lying to your company is like lying to your lawyer or doctor—it just hurts you in the end.

I always tell my team, "When you see a turd, clean it up." Otherwise, it starts smelling up the whole place. There is no point in ignoring or hiding the truth. You know it's there, and pretty soon, everyone else will, too.

If an employee at NTM makes an error—well, it happens. Sometimes those little errors have costly consequences, but that's part of life and being human. I consider these mistakes to be the cost of doing business. We always tell our customers when we make a mistake and then immediately lay out a plan for how we'll fix it. We don't dodge responsibility or come up with some bullshit excuse. And every time, I take the fall and the final responsibility for my employees' mistakes. I joke with my employees that everyone gets one big mistake per year. First one's on me, second one's on you. Usually, they don't make the same mistake twice because they learn quickly in the supportive environment we've created at NTM. They know they won't get shit from me. They're not going to get yelled at or made fun of. But if you lie to me, or do something illegal or immoral, you're out. The same goes for customers. If you're straight with me, I'll bend over backward for you. If you try to fuck with me, goodbye.

This doesn't mean I don't have empathy for people who have problems that lead them to hide their issues or outright lie, but that empathy comes with healthy boundaries. I had to fire an employee a while back for his continued drinking and drug use. But that didn't mean I stopped caring about him. After he had a drunk driving accident, I helped him get into rehab. Only once I had set him up with support did I fire him. He accused me of abandoning him, which was painful to hear. I was holding him accountable for his actions. Recently, I ran into him at an event we both attended. I thought he wanted to fight me, but instead, he gave me a big hug and thanked me. He got clean, got back with his baby's mother, bought a house, and started a company.

Being real with people doesn't always result in changed lives and new relationships evolving out of old ones, but when it does, it's incredibly rewarding. Honesty and integrity provide a solid foundation for improving communication and outcomes.

CHAPTER THREE

COMMUNICATION

"If you weren't my aunt, I'd fuck the shit out of you."

I didn't understand why the entire room fell silent because I was utterly wasted. I didn't notice everyone cringe and shake their heads, awkwardly looking around for an escape. I didn't register the hurt and embarrassment on my aunt's face, who'd been a kind presence and role model in my life. I'd humiliated her in front of almost one hundred of my friends and family members at my fortieth birthday party.

The next morning, I woke up hungover and immediately started drinking again before I dragged myself to a meeting with a customer who promptly fired me. I got a call from my uncle, telling me that the night before had been a total disaster and asking what in the world was I thinking to make such an ass out of myself and humiliate his wife in front of everyone. I spent the rest of the morning calling my aunt and every guest who had been at the party to apologize for my unacceptable behavior. Unfortunately, that horrible evening is memorialized on video, and rewatching my speech is mortifying. I realized the morning after my birthday party that my problem with alcohol impacted my communication to the extent of damaging my relationships.

In this chapter, I'll share the mistakes I've made and the resources I've used to improve my communication. As we'll discuss, becoming self-aware and focusing on honesty and integrity have made a big difference in how I communicate now, but consistent evolution is the key ingredient.

COMMUNICATION STARTS WITH US

One of the hardest conversations I've ever had was in therapy. It was an imaginary conversation with my stepdad and mom about how they treated little Kelly. It was a conversation prompted by my therapist to advocate for my inner child as my adult self. Yes, I know it sounds ridiculous, but hear me out. I could barely ask why they treated little Kelly so cruelly before bursting out in tears. The emotions were completely overwhelming, and I felt a seething rage toward my parents. I wanted to strangle them.

The way they treated me and talked to me left scars and impacted how I talked to myself for decades. I used to call myself a dumb, old hillbilly who just knows how to sell. I didn't have the confidence to be who I truly am, and that was reflected in the words I used to describe myself. I'm a highly educated, functional, kind, vulnerable guy still processing the pain of my past.

I now realize that I can be both badass and sensitive, successful and struggling, strong and vulnerable. Now, how I talk about myself and to myself reflects the complexity of being human. I allow myself to feel the pain of my past, while appreciating the lessons I've learned.

Sometimes I still wonder if I'm ugly or stupid or unlovable, but I know that's my stepdad talking. I can't eliminate that inner critic, but I can redirect that voice and actively replace it with more accepting and compassionate language. Usually, we think of communication in terms of how we talk to others, but it starts with how we talk to ourselves.

BIG HAT, NO CATTLE

Communication is meaningless if you don't back it up with action. I used to turn into an asshole when I was drunk and say mean things to people I cared about. Sometimes, like my uncle, they would tell me how I insulted them, and I'd apologize. I figured that was enough, then I'd turn around and get drunk again the next day.

Nobody cares about apologies if they're never followed by a change in behavior. I tried to blame my behavior and terrible moods on stress at work, problems with my girlfriend, or whatever other bullshit excuse I could come up with. The truth is, it was all me.

Just like your apologies are meaningless without change, so are your promises if you continually break them. My aunt forgave me, but my actions in the following years mattered much more than words. It took another three years for me to quit drinking, but since then, I've not only made verbal amends but also shown that I'm changing my behavior to match my actions to my words.

BECOME A BETTER COMMUNICATOR

We often think communication means talking, and we all know how to talk, so what is there to learn? I've found that educating myself about how to communicate more effectively and practicing different communication styles takes effort. Even though I have the gift of gab and can talk to anyone about anything, I want to optimize how I communicate. With this goal in mind, I've devoured lots of helpful resources and books on the topic.

One of my favorite books, *The Four Agreements* by Don Miguel Ruiz, offers excellent advice about communication that I practice daily: be impeccable with your word and don't make assumptions. This advice addresses both sides of the communication—what I say and how I listen. I'm very careful to say only what I mean and always mean what I say, to make sure my communication is as clear and honest as possible. And I also don't assume to know what the other person means, so I deploy curiosity and openness. I practice listening to others to hear what they're saying, not whatever story I've already made up in my head.

Never Split the Difference by former FBI hostage negotiator Chris Voss helped me understand that, too often, I did split the difference. Making deals was so important to me that I agreed to compromises that weren't profitable for me or only in the customer's best interest. Voss explains different communication techniques to handle high-stakes negotiations that help avoid power struggles and create win-win agreements. I now approach negotiations with that mindset, communicating boundaries respectfully but firmly. I've learned that walking away from a bad deal is often better in the long run.

Marshall Rosenberg's *Nonviolent Communication* taught me

that, while it's important to be open and vulnerable in communication, it's also important to stay emotionally steady. It's counter-productive, and even damaging, to communicate when highly emotional. If you feel like cussing someone out, screaming, or completely shutting down, you must first regulate those emotions before attempting to communicate with anyone else.

INVITE HONEST COMMUNICATION

Nobody will communicate with you honestly if they feel you don't welcome their feedback. Especially, if you're the boss and control people's livelihoods. First, seek to understand before desiring to be understood.

In a conversation with my leadership team about two underperforming employees, I couldn't get a straight answer from my team regarding the best way to deal with these staff members. I bluntly stated that they needed to be let go. My leadership team sighed in relief because they didn't want to be the bearer of bad news, especially because I care so much about every employee and personally hurt if I need to fire anyone. However, that doesn't make me blind to the fact that someone may be wrong for their position or our company.

What bothered me more about this situation is that my leadership team didn't give it to me straight. I could say it was their fault because they didn't have the courage, but it's more productive to consider what I can do better as a leader to encourage open communication. If I'm always talking and rarely listening, I will miss moments when my team could be honest with me. If I'm judgmental, loud, and harsh, I'm not creating psychological safety for my team to come to me with hard truths. No, I'm not talking about safe spaces for overly sensitive people with a victim complex. I'm talking about the fact that psychological safety is a prerequisite for honest communication. If it's not safe to be honest with me because I might become angry or dismissive or punish my employees for their honesty, I'm not creating an environment of psychological safety.

I've always been big, loud, and brash. That sometimes works against me when I need my team to trust they can bring anything and everything to me. Listening and curiosity are what I'm focusing on right now to ensure this aspect of my leadership skills grows.

CURIOSITY IN COMMUNICATION

Like my dad, I'm genuinely interested in other people. I love a great discussion, a passionate debate, a deep conversation. I'm sincerely fascinated by figuring out what makes people tick. People who are only comfortable with superficial conversations or who have a lot of unhealed trauma may feel uneasy or awkward with my incessant questions. However, I'm not judging them. I'm just curious, asking questions to get to know others and figure out how I can be of service.

This goes for both personal and professional communication. I believe this is a skill everyone can benefit from, and I strive to instill it in my team. I recently noticed that a colleague was talking over people and reminded them that an important part of effective leadership is holding space for our work family members. I want everyone to feel valued and heard. When I was still drinking, I would have never, ever considered the importance of this. Instead, I would have rolled my eyes at such fluff. It was kill or be killed, and that was reflected in my communications with others, both at home and at work. Now instead of barking orders, I ask questions. Instead of being prescriptive, I'm curious. Instead of being dismissive, I'm genuinely interested.

At my bachelor party, before getting married for the first time at twenty-four, my uncle had a talk with me. He asked me questions: *Are you sure this is what you want to do? She's a great girl, but are you ready for this commitment?* Years later, long after that marriage had ended, I asked my uncle if he had been trying to talk me out of getting married. *I was, Kelly,* he replied, *but I knew you wouldn't listen if you didn't feel like it was your idea.* My uncle's wisdom stuck with me. Nobody likes to be told what to do. That's why it's better to be curious and try to understand the other person's perspective. If they're ready to listen, a question might get them to reconsider their position. And if they're not ready to listen, there's nothing you or I can do anyway to change their mind.

TALK LESS, LISTEN MORE

I got the gift of gab. I love people. I love selling. But more and more, I realize how important listening is. As the saying goes, there's a reason we were made with one mouth and two ears. My dad was such a great example of an excellent listener, and I strive to emulate him. In some ways, learning to be a better listener is harder than quitting drinking for me. It sounds extreme, but it's true. Whenever I walk out of a meeting where I've rambled on without giving anyone else the chance to speak, I ask myself *why*. I don't want to dominate every conversation. When I was still drinking, I pretended to listen, but I was just waiting for my turn to speak. I listened to reply, not to hear and understand someone else. Now, I genuinely care about other people's opinions and ideas. And yet, I still frequently can't stop myself from talking incessantly.

The more I dig into the habits and behaviors that are difficult for me to break, the more I realize they are old survival mechanisms. When I was younger, talking created a buffer and often kept me from getting beaten. I knew that if I kept my mom and stepdad talking, I could buy time and figure out my next step. I could distract them, divert their attention, keep them engaged, or do whatever else I needed to do to defuse volatile situations.

Of course, my team will not beat me up if I don't talk my way through an entire meeting, but my long-standing habit of rambling automatically kicks in whenever I feel uneasy or nervous. There are many personal and professional situations when these feelings crop up. It takes a conscious effort to remind myself I'm not in a life-and-death situation. It's safe to be quiet and just listen.

Once I realized how many of my default behaviors were holdover coping mechanisms to deal with childhood trauma, it was easier to stop judging myself and, instead, focus on making a new behavior stick.

HOW TO HAVE HARD CONVERSATIONS

Don't put off difficult conversations. The conversations will not get easier the longer you wait. Just do the damn thing. Call the person. Better yet, talk to them face-to-face. The more anxiety you have, the more important it is to get it out. There is no perfect way to handle situations like this, so initiate the conversation and then shut up and listen. Try to listen with an open heart, curiosity, and compassion. Don't lecture, judge, or give unsolicited advice.

The truth hurts once, but a lie hurts forever. Sometimes we lie to "protect" ourselves or others, but in doing so, we inadvertently create more problems down the road. It's important to be as kind and gentle as possible when speaking the truth—but it still must be spoken. Don't beat around the bush. Don't sugarcoat the problem. It helps to keep things short, focused on the facts, and solution-oriented. I got no time to play the blame game. Here's the problem, now what are we going to do to fix it?

I'm telling you stuff I've been telling myself. Selling requires a lot of talking, so while I've focused on talking, my listening skills have suffered. Parenting a teenage daughter, building my business, and becoming sober have all helped me understand the power of deep listening and seeking to understand why people do what they do, how they think, and what their motives are.

I practice listening every day because I want my daughter to speak freely to me about anything she's struggling with. I want my employees to tell me hard truths so we can all make the company better together. I want to cultivate friendships in which I listen when a buddy tells me what I need to hear, rather than what I want to hear. And I want to have a romantic relationship at some point that is fortified by trust and respect, following Brené Brown's advice that "clarity is kindness."

CONFLICT RESOLUTION

If there's an issue on my team, I avoid texts and emails at all costs. I call an in-person meeting or a video conference. I don't want anyone to hide behind a screen, and I don't want misunderstandings to occur due to not seeing people's body language or hearing their tone of voice.

I first make sure that everyone agrees on the goal of the meeting. That goal should be a tangible outcome that fixes a problem, not a personal vendetta with the aim of proving someone else wrong. Winners fix problems, losers assign blame.

Once we've agreed on the objective goal, I listen to everyone tell their side of the situation. I don't interrupt unless things get heated and someone goes off the rails or throws around insults or obscenities. Often the issue is not what we're discussing, but an underlying problem nobody has named yet. Hearing everyone out often brings the real issue to the surface. Then we process that problem before trying to address any solutions.

TAKE RESPONSIBILITY FOR YOUR PART

A year into my sobriety, I had a meeting with a client that ended up in a screaming match with him storming out of the office. I was sure they'd cancel the contract as a result, but they didn't. The CEO and I had a frank conversation after we both calmed down, and each of us took responsibility for the way we handled the discussion.

Being on a journey of personal progress doesn't mean I'll never mess up. It just means that I'll fess up and fix my part. Luckily, in this situation, the other CEO was open and honest enough to do the same, and we had a productive conversation as a result. When the contract renewal came due, we had already set the stage for honest communication. They told us they were shopping around for a vendor and the gaps they needed us to fill in our service coverage. We got back with a realistic plan and budget and worked out an expanded contract that's a win-win for everyone. I believe this was all possible because honest communication builds trust and respect.

COMMUNICATION AND PARENTING

My dad passed away a long time ago, but I still miss talking to him. Every day, I come across at least one situation that makes me think of him and feel the urge to ask for his advice. If I could only pick his brain about business decisions or parenting issues. It may seem weird, considering that my dad abandoned me for his alcohol and drug addictions. But he also talked to me like I was his equal, even when I was a child. He never spoke to me in that condescending, patronizing tone that so many parents take with their children. He had a lot of issues, but he was honest and real, accepting and nonjudgmental, and that always came through in his communication.

My mom and stepdad's way of "communicating" was the opposite of this. They either ignored me or told me how stupid and worthless I was. Communication consisted of screaming insults and barking orders. Conversation wasn't encouraged, and any that did occur was considered "talking back" and "being disrespectful." I lived for the weekends when I spent time with my dad and grandparents, who encouraged me to talk around the dinner table, shared stories with me, asked me questions, and were genuinely curious about my answers.

I try my best to do the same with Arianna. She's smart, kind, and capable, and that's how I talk to her, whether we're sitting down for dinner, walking the dog, or going out on the boat. As she's turning into a young woman, I'm trying my hardest to level with her and keep the lines of communication open.

EVOLVING COMMUNICATION PATTERNS

Before I quit drinking, I was much more impatient in my communication. I was the bull in the china shop, tearing the whole place apart with my aggressive and reckless communication style. I thought saying whatever I wanted was keeping it real, no matter how hurtful. I confused my callousness with brutal honesty, and even took pride in it.

I believed the saying *in vino veritas* (in wine lies the truth), pretending I was more honest and truthful when drunk. The reality, of course, is that I just talked a bunch of nonsensical gibberish while drunk, so people stopped listening to my ramblings.

Learning how to improve my communication has helped me tremendously in my professional life and navigating my family relationships.

CHAPTER FOUR

FAMILY

"Fix it! Fix it!" my mother screamed while throwing punches at me. As she landed a fist square on my nose, the shooting pain filled my eyes with tears.

"I can't, Mom!" I yelled, trying to get out of my room, where she'd cornered me. It was my eighth birthday.

I've hated my birthday for as long as I can remember. One of my earliest memories is waking up on my fifth birthday to my mom and stepdad telling me they didn't get me any presents. I went back to my room and bawled my eyes out, only to hear my mom and stepdad bust out laughing. I slowly realized they'd pranked me as they pulled out an electric train set, cowboy hat, and toy pistols. The thing is, I wasn't surprised when they said they didn't get me anything because I didn't expect kindness from them. Today I know they weren't fit parents because of their alcohol and drug addictions. Back then, I just thought they didn't love me. I can tell myself now that they didn't know better. They thought it was funny. And still, decades later, I think about what a rotten thing that was to do to a little boy.

Although my fifth birthday was epically shitty, it was only downhill from there. To my recollection, it was the last one of my birthdays anyone in my house celebrated as my mom and stepdad slipped deeper into alcohol and pill addictions. That's why I couldn't believe my luck when I turned eight. Although my dad struggled with substance abuse just like my mom and stepdad, he was still functioning at that time. He'd pick me up most weekends to spend time with me. He was my hero in a world where heroes were hard to come by. He took me out for a birthday treat and bought me a Walkman. I'm sure that Walkman was a $10 piece of junk, but it didn't matter. My dad cared. He bought me a present. I was so happy that I got to escape the hellhole my home had become. I listened to my new Walkman nonstop and fell asleep wearing it after he dropped me back off at home.

In the middle of the night, I was startled awake by my mother, who'd forgotten it was my birthday but saw me sleeping with the Walkman. I knew she was drunk; I could smell it on her. She demanded to use the Walkman. I didn't know that I'd accidentally broken off one of the plastic earpieces while lying in bed with it. My mom grew more agitated as I groggily tried to reattach the earpiece. When the Walkman still didn't work, she pushed me angrily, insisting I fix it. I scrambled out of bed and away from her, but she chased me around the room, and started beating me viciously. I couldn't see through my tears and blood, as I desperately tried to escape her fists. I knew she would beat me to death over a broken Walkman if I didn't get out of my room and away from her. The last thing I remember is stumbling out of my room, hearing the sound of a door opening, and my sister stepping out to punch my mom back and then grabbing my limp body. She dragged me into her room and locked the door behind us.

My sister was nine years older than me and had received her share of beatings until she reached out to a social worker who removed her from our house. She still came over to visit me sometimes, and usually spent the night. It was pure luck she was there that night. Later, my sister gave me her social worker's number and told me, "You gotta get out of this fucking house, Kelly. One of these days, she's going to kill you." She had talked to the social worker about getting me out multiple times, but they kept telling her I had to make a statement myself. I never called the social worker, although my sister begged me to. I was too afraid of what my mom and stepdad might do to me if I told anyone about the abuse. This was over three decades ago. Things were different then.

Finally, after getting into a fight with my stepdad eight years later, when I was sixteen, I threw my clothes into a couple of garbage bags and left early one morning. I didn't take anything besides my clothes and some personal items. I wanted nothing from my childhood home. I moved in with my sister and her husband until I finished high school. She saved my life in more ways than one.

Being generous and giving others thoughtful gifts is important to me, but I haven't figured out how to openly receive gifts myself. I've only started practicing this now, at forty-six. I still hate my birthday and don't like getting gifts. If I want something, I'll get it for myself. I never again want to be in a situation where I hope to receive something from someone else only to be disappointed. And when I do get a thoughtful gift or am extended a kindness, I find myself waiting for the other shoe to drop. I've learned to never get too high or too low because the seasons change, and there is some inherent unpredictability in everyone. These birthdays really did a number on me, and ever since I've questioned whether or not I'm good enough and worthy of love.

Family is my priority, precisely because I grew up in such a violent, toxic home environment. By processing my childhood trauma, I strive to create the family I wish I'd had myself.

CHOSEN FAMILY—BUILT ON TRUST, NOT BLOOD

As my uncle says: "You can pick your nose, but you can't pick your family." While that sentiment is true about biological families, we all have the option of creating chosen families, based on trust, not blood. Early on, I understood the importance of making and keeping good friends because, growing up, my friends *were* my family. We played sports, ran the streets, and were fiercely loyal to each other. Of course, friends are also a big reason why I started drinking. Everyone was doing it, and we were all escaping broken, dysfunctional homes in one way or another. I wanted to belong with my chosen family. While they all had their issues, some of them became "moving friends"— the ones who will show up to help when you have to pack up your life, without being bribed with beer and pizza.

It took decades and some emotional distance to realize how my family of origin was toxic. I used to wonder why my mother didn't love me. Why did my dad abandon me? Why didn't my stepdad accept me? All those things made me who I am, but they also hurt like hell. I looked for the reason within myself until I read a book that opened my eyes. It was called *Toxic Parents: Overcoming Their Hurtful Legacy and Reclaiming Your Life* by Susan Forward and explained different dysfunctional family systems and parenting styles. That book explained to me for the first time what it meant to have addicted, inadequate, neglectful, and abusive parents. I called my sister, read parts of the book to her, and asked if the descriptions of those toxic family systems resonated with her. It was validating to hear that we had similar experiences and perspectives on our parents. It didn't change how much their behavior hurt, but it alleviated my tendency to take the blame for my parents' behavior. I understood that I hadn't deserved their treatment, and that their abuse and addiction were never about me. The responsibility was theirs alone.

FAMILY IS WHAT MAKES A HOUSE A HOME

Because the house I grew up in wasn't a home, I've always put a lot of importance on making my own place warm and welcoming. Over the years, I went from sneaking out of my mom and stepdad's house in the early morning hours with only a couple of garbage bags to my name to relying on my "moving friends" to help me move my belongings to my first condo. The next time I moved, I could afford hiring professional movers, and after building my second home in Florida recently, I was able to purchase all new furniture. This isn't to brag; it's to remind myself where I've come from and how much hard work it took to get where I am.

After my dad died when I was twenty-three, I used the small inheritance he left me for a down payment on a condo to make a fresh start. My relationship with my dad had been fraught, especially during the last years of his life, when he was imprisoned in his addictions. It hurt when I had to throw him out of my grandparents' house because he was drunk and belligerent. After that incident, I didn't speak to him again until I said my last goodbyes.

The condo was not just a home but the place where I would start my company, then called Kelly Communications. I was still working full-time at my day job as a salesman for a telecommunication company, and working on my business nights and weekends, but my dad's gift (and a couple of maxed-out credit cards) helped me launch my new life.

When I decided to quit my day job and devote myself to my company full time, I moved out of that condo and into my first real house with my then-wife. I thought it would be my forever home. My two best "moving friends," Mike and Steve, came over and helped me pack up the condo and move everything over to my house in a single day. Although that house didn't turn out to be forever, it still holds significance for me because of all the family memories, both good and bad, packed into it. The house was big and had a pool, so I always invited friends and family over to hang out and party. I finally got a piece of the good life and wanted to share it with the people I loved. It was a lot of fun, but it was also a time of excess. People were coming in and out, the house was trashed from parties nearly every weekend, and some of my family and friends started taking advantage of my hospitality and generosity.

I stayed in that house for thirteen years, during which Kelly Communications became National Technology Management

(NTM). But first, I turned into a huge drinker, watched my marriage fall apart, experienced the betrayal of friends and family, and finally became sober. When I moved out of that house, I cried because it's the place where I became me.

Today I prefer to hang around people who can afford movers. Hey, I'm forty-six, and I'm not going to throw out my back just so you can save a couple of bucks! But back in the day, when my friends and I were young and broke, we showed up for each other as family, and we still do. We can afford to hire movers now, but our friendship has stayed the same. To this day, they're my family. I recently hosted Steve's fiftieth birthday party at my house in Florida, celebrating and reminiscing about how far we've come together.

I've lived in thirteen different homes. After growing up in chaos, I finally have a sense of stability and security. I'm proud of building a solid home for my daughter—the safe, loving place I always lacked. This stability results in peace, which allows me to make progress, and that's exactly what I want for Ari, too.

LIVING THE GOOD LIFE CHANGED MY RELATIONSHIPS

That "less than" feeling instilled in me growing up in South Warren is a motherfucker to overcome. I empathize with the people I grew up with who are still poor, addicted, and stuck. I know what it feels like because I've been there. However, I still had to learn how to set healthy boundaries with people who were jealous of my success or tried to exploit me.

I first noticed that people were uncomfortable with my material success when NTM started taking off. One day, I invited my sister's husband Ed on my boat to hang out and have a good time. I tried to keep it light and fun, but he started grilling me about money and why I was working so hard. He was shocked when I told him how much it cost to cover my monthly expenses and how many hours I put in to pay for that lifestyle. To him, the amount of money I made and spent every month to live the life I wanted was ridiculous. It seemed outrageous to him, but it's all relative. My life is affordable compared to other people. More importantly, I won't apologize for the success I've had so far, and what I'm working toward now. It doesn't mean I'm looking down on my brother-in-law or anyone else in my extended family who doesn't have as much material success. At the same time, I won't hide that I'm proud of what I've accomplished and made of myself.

Before growing up and marrying my sister, Ed was our neighbor. He was always good to me, and I consider him instrumental in making me who I am today. When I had to leave my mom's house, he welcomed me into his home that he shared with my sister, no questions asked. He gave me a place to live and encouraged me to finish school. But over the years, our relationship deteriorated. When their son, my nephew Eddie Jr., came out as gay, I got into a massive fight with Ed. He'd been drinking and raged about Eddie tarnishing his good name. My sister had to separate us before the spat got physical. My relationships with both my sister and Ed have been strained ever since.

When I hosted parties every weekend in my first home, I thought the people around me were my friends and family. I thought being family meant having drinking buddies who didn't judge my excess and bailed me out when I needed them. It was years before I realized how quickly they'd scatter once I quit drinking.

I let people I considered family use my house and pool but then found myself alone, cleaning up their crushed beer cans, filling up the pool, and restocking my fridge. There was no gratitude for my generosity, and definitely no reciprocity.

I slowly realized that the people I trusted were using me for material comforts and didn't respect how hard I worked for that house. I didn't get all this shit from winning at a quiz show! I worked my ass off to get to where I was, pulling twelve-hour days on the regular, without even stopping for lunch. I could not understand why nobody was "leaving the woodpile a little higher"—a mantra I always tried to follow myself.

One day my nephew Eddie called me up while I was on my boat, asking if he could come over to hang out with me. I told him *next time*, since I was out. When I came home later that day, I found my nephew hosting a rager at my house. I was angry about his lie and sad about his betrayal. He hadn't called because he wanted to spend time with me. He called to make sure I was gone so he could use my house, swim in my pool, and drink all my beer with his buddies. He left the entire place trashed.

I understand we all do stupid shit when we're young, drunk, or both. But I 'fessed up to all the dumb shit I did, and I expect the same from anyone in my life, with or without substance abuse issues. I had to tell my nephew that he could no longer come to my house whenever he wanted because I couldn't trust him and would not be lied to. He is still welcome in my home when I'm there, but he hasn't shown up since that party. He has never apologized or taken responsibility.

SETTING BOUNDARIES WITH FAMILY

One of my biggest regrets is not being able to make my relationship with my nephew work, but eventually, I had to set boundaries. I still love and care for all of the friends and family members I've had to set boundaries with, but I had to make some changes for my mental health. I still wish I could do more for people, especially my sister, whom I leaned on throughout my childhood. I wouldn't have made it out alive if it hadn't been for her.

For a while after I first achieved some financial success, I was asked for money or to co-sign loans so often that I've had to make a hard rule not to loan money to my family. People get funny when money is involved. Families fight over inheritances, of course, but money can also damage relationships when everyone is still alive.

I'm happy to support, mentor, and help anyone who is serious about changing their situation, but I won't be used and exploited. It's hard to overcome our families and communities telling us that we're nothing. Getting stuck in that hamster wheel of self-hate and self-pity is easy. It takes a lot to break the cycle. My sister is a much better mom than our mother, so she broke the cycle in that way. Eddie is a good kid. I'm proud of him, and I'm proud of my sister, but at the same time, I'm also sad because I know they're capable of so much more. They don't believe it, though, and I can't make them.

It's easy to fall into a victim mentality, but that way of life drives me nuts. I can't be around people who only whine and complain and never want to lift a finger to change their circumstances.

Recently I made the difficult decision to cut off one of my dearest friends, Ray. I let him live in my Florida house for six weeks rent-free so that he could get away from his regular stomping grounds and dry out. I have compassion for his struggles with alcoholism, and I've tried for years to help him get out of that vicious cycle, but he just keeps spinning out. He doesn't yet realize that he's on a sinking ship. Nothing I did to help him worked. He kept disrespecting my house, calling me names, and generally acting like an ass. I gave him second, third, and fourth chances because I saw myself in him, but my patience eventually wore out. Taking care of myself is not selfish. It's necessary to stay mentally healthy and to continue being able to support the people who want help and are willing to make positive changes.

I've finally stopped caring what anyone thinks of me, family or not, because I won't be dragged down with them. I stopped seeking people's approval so I could start building the life and family I truly want.

TREATING EMPLOYEES LIKE FAMILY

When COVID hit, the first thing I did was check my personal and business accounts to see how long I could pay all of my employees. Everyone I allow in my orbit is treated like family, so this was my first order of business. My employees aren't just workers, but people with hopes, dreams, and families. It makes me happy to have seen six of my employees buy houses, three people get married, and one of my employee's kids graduate from college and get his first real job. I was happy to set up some interviews and help this young person get a head start. My staff are my family, and their families are my extended family. We're part of each other's lives, and they all know I deeply care about them.

We recently implemented EOS, the Entrepreneurial Operating System, which will help us supercharge the business and attract high-achievers to the team. EOS is a comprehensive blueprint for running a successful company, and includes a component for building high-performing teams. EOS allows us to rank our existing employees and then offer them opportunities to adapt their performance. If they are unwilling to change, we will let them go. I finally delegated this process to my executive team because I could tell I was too emotionally invested in my relationships with staff. I had a hard time letting them go, even if I knew I needed to. While I will storm over anyone who gets in my way, I also have a soft spot for the people I consider family. I've overcome a lot to be the boring, winning, bad motherfucker I am today, and I lead by example. But I can only do so much. Ultimately, I need to make decisions that are best for the business and everyone working for me. Hell, I threw my own dad out of my grandparents' house because it needed to be done. I love hard, but you don't want to get in my way and try to drag my whole team down with you. I'll cut you off no matter how much it hurts. So, we're making some changes at NTM, and not everyone will survive them.

My employees know I love them even if I have to let them go. Less than an hour after my executive team had to fire Brad, a long-term employee, he texted me to say he still loved me like family and always would. I feel the same, which is why it's so hard for me to demote or fire people when they don't perform. It's tough because I know this is Brad's livelihood. I care for him as a person, but it finally got to the point where I had to make the best decision for the company and set some boundaries. I wish I didn't have to demonstrate that level of tough love, but stats don't lie. The EOS we're implementing to track metrics very clearly told my executive team that his performance wasn't up to snuff, and that he showed no willingness to improve his work. When others were resolving twenty to thirty support tickets a day, he was touching one. The writing was on the wall, and everyone knew what was coming.

Brad made excuses for why he couldn't do the work, that he was doing bigger and better things, and that working tickets was beneath him. That's not how NTM works, though. We're a family, and we're all in this together. Nobody is above any task. If I'm crawling under desks installing hardware, you better not be too fancy to work support tickets. The thing is, Brad was our smartest, most qualified engineer. I let him go because our company culture and working together as a team toward common goals are more important to me than giving a pass to one intelligent guy who could do fantastic work but chooses not to.

Everything I do, every decision I make, is with the intention of getting better in business and life. I tried encouraging Brad to do the same, but he didn't. We talk a lot about winning every day at work, but Brad never caught on. He was slacking at work, neglecting his health, obsessed with gaming, and unwilling to do anything to better his life. I had to remind him of his wedding anniversary every year because he usually forgot. No matter how much I cared about Brad, he was not aligned with the values of NTM that I model in my personal and professional life. He didn't try to be his best self. He didn't take life seriously. He's only thirty, so hopefully, he'll take this as a wake-up call that he can't just do the bare minimum and coast his entire life.

Part of the issue, of course, is that for most of my time leading

NTM, I was a drunk. When I was drinking and partying, I didn't give a shit if I lived or died. I said fuck it; I'll go out at forty-six like my dad. Many of my clients and staff who drank with or around me couldn't perform at the same level as I did while drunk. Once I got sober, it became obvious that these clients or employees couldn't keep up with me. I had to fire clients as well as employees.

Brad is just the most recent example. I had several clients who not only loved to do business with me but also loved to party with me. One guy in particular, Dean, became a good buddy. I thought we were friends, but we were just two drunks commiserating. Once I quit drinking, he not only stopped doing business with me, but our friendship fizzled out quickly, too. It felt like a betrayal on both levels. There'd been times at work when I'd come in hungover and didn't bring my A-game. I was embarrassed of myself. I thought getting sober would improve my relationships and that others would be happy with the change. I quickly realized that my newfound sobriety made people uncomfortable. I was more present and aware. I held myself to a higher standard, and everyone else, too. Many people didn't like that.

I want to surround myself with people in my personal and professional life who are positive, driven, and growth-focused. I want my employees to take care of their physical, emotional, and mental health for themselves, but also so they can bring their A-game to work. While NTM has existed for decades, the first few years of my sobriety and my focus on personal progress have allowed me to make drastic changes to our company culture. People who are used to drunk Kelly may never be willing to buy into the new culture I'm creating. That's unfortunate but to be expected. NTM was great before, but it's time to level up, and I need people on my team who share my vision.

My personal and professional progress and success are intertwined. I would not be able to hold space for Brad and be compassionate for his situation if I didn't do my personal development work. It helps me have hard conversations and make tough decisions while still showing genuine empathy. In the past, I would have felt guilty and doubted my decision to let Brad go. I can grieve losing a member of my work family and still know that I absolutely did the right thing for myself and my company.

I always have hope that people get on the personal progress bandwagon. I focus a lot on continuing education for my staff because I believe in continuous growth and improvement at every level. Not everyone takes advantage of it, but I lead by example and hope my employees follow suit. I have two employees I love dearly who haven't been receptive to my new approach at NTM. I've had to demote them and put them on a performance plan. As of this writing, Matt has been let go, but Jim has adapted and is thriving. I doubt Matt will read this book because he's not necessarily personal progress-minded (Hey Matt, I changed your name to protect the guilty, but you know who you are. If you've actually picked up this book, give me a holler, and I'll give you $100, but I'm pretty sure that money is staying right where it is).

As with my personal relationships, I realized many of my employees were also stuck in that victim mentality while I moved on to creating my own universe. Because I see my work family as my real family, I'm very cautious now when hiring. There are many steps to our recruitment process, and the last one is a lengthy interview with me that has little to do with work and everything to do with life. I put together twenty-three questions I got from Mike Metcalf and Shaun Peet's book *12 Second Culture*. These questions cover professional and personal topics and help me get to know the person I'm about to bring into my work family. I need to make sure candidates not only have the professional chops but are also like-minded personalities who are a good fit for our team. We're in a hiring phase right now because we're focusing on EOS and getting people in place who are excited about NTM's trajectory and aligned with our values. You can find the complete list of questions in Appendix B.

WHAT FAMILY MEANS TO ME NOW

Family is about building relationships based on trust, not blood. These relationships thrive on honesty, loyalty, communication, and growth. I don't believe that blood is thicker than water, and while I can't choose my biological family, I can pick my chosen family.

Even the best family will face difficulties, but communication and working together allow me to have a small but tight family. Family is not just about celebrating the good times but also having each other's backs when the going gets tough. We are there for each other, no matter what. My late grandma and my aunt have always been there for me and mothered me when my own mother couldn't or wouldn't. They rarely asked me for help, but when they did, I'd jump at the opportunity to repay some of the kindnesses they showered me with over the years. Whether it's replacing light bulbs or carrying heavy furniture, I'm there, no questions asked, if they need anything.

My aunt especially has had a lot of patience with me. Remember the story about my fortieth birthday? I was so ashamed that I embarrassed her in front of everyone, especially because she's always done right by me and was one of my biggest supporters. Of course, she'd lectured me about quitting drinking, and for decades, I didn't listen. She still loved me unconditionally and never gave up on me. She was full of pride and joy when I finally decided to stop. Now, I can give back to her and her family and show my appreciation for everything she's done for me. Today, my family is made up of some blood and some chosen members who've been there for me through the good, the bad, and the ugly.

I enjoy my small, close-knit ride-or-die family and my circle of extended family and friends. But I still spend an excessive amount of time alone. I'd rather be by myself than with anyone inauthentic or people who drain my energy, like negative Nellies or people with victim mentalities. Especially after I quit drinking, I started making sure that I only allow people into my orbit who I truly consider family and that I protect my energy at all costs.

HOW I BUILT THE FAMILY I ALWAYS WANTED

To build the family I wanted, I first needed to understand the family I came from. The more I focused on self-awareness and personal progress, the more I understood how my childhood home and family life impacts me still today. For the longest time, I didn't know why I always felt edgy toward the end of the weekend. I was successful professionally and had no reason to dread Mondays. My morning routine, including exercise and meditation, was the same every day. My weekends were usually full of quality time with my daughter or friends.

I finally figured out that for most of my childhood, I whiplashed back and forth between being scared to death all week while living with violent alcoholics (my mom and stepdad), and getting a reprieve on weekends with my dad before he descended deeper into his own addiction. Those weekends were usually filled with quality time, conversation, and visits to my grandparents' house. The extremes and instability of my family situation had me going from terror to joy, neglect to attention, violence to affection, over and over. I never realized how stressful that was for me as a little boy and how it stuck with me as a grown-ass man, leading me to feel anxious, worried, and edgy at the end of every weekend.

This is only one example of how I'm slowly unpacking the way my childhood family dynamics shaped me, and how they've influenced how I create my own family life with my daughter. I don't believe the saying "I am who I am." Bullshit. You are who you learned to be. Unlearn that shit! We're all taught to be a certain way by our families, peers, and community, but we don't have to stay that way. We have control over our lives and the families we create.

When I'm asked how I parent my daughter and create the family I always wanted and never had, my advice sounds so simple it's almost ridiculous, but it works for me. My mom and stepdad were so dysfunctional and abusive that I literally just do the opposite of whatever they did. I was constantly yelled at, so I make an effort to lower my voice. I didn't get unconditional love, so I shower Arianna with love. Nobody ever told me they loved me, so I say it to her every day. I text my sister that I love her, which often makes me cry and cringe because I'm so uncomfortable. Not because it's not true, but because there was no love in our house, and we weren't taught to express affection to each other. If it's uncomfortable, it probably means I'm growing, so I lean into that shit.

Since my family forgot most of my birthdays, I make a big deal out of Ari's birthday. Her thirteenth birthday certainly was very different from mine. I took her out to a fancy dinner and treated her all day. Nothing will keep me from my daughter on her birthday.

The only thing I didn't do the opposite of was drink. I did spend my entire adult life until three years ago drinking, just like my parents. It's one of the reasons I talk to my daughter about drinking, just like my father spoke to me about serious topics. One thing I learned from my dad and still do with my daughter is talk eye-to-eye, like adults. Before my father got swallowed up in his substance abuse, he came around every weekend to pick me up and spend time with me when I was between the ages of five and thirteen. Like I said, he always talked to me like an equal, and I deeply appreciated that. It's something I try to emulate in my relationship with Ari. She's a teen now, and I hope she will wait to experiment with drugs and alcohol. I try not to talk down to her about these topics. I hope she takes my advice and experience with alcohol seriously and learns from it without having to make all the same mistakes I did. Smart people learn from their mistakes, wise people learn from other people's mistakes. Either way, I will be there for her.

I still mess up, of course. The other day I yelled at my daughter for quitting track. I know it's hard to be my kid. I'm a bit of a perfectionist and sometimes ask for too much. I was mad that she quit on her team. She wasn't impeccable with her word, which is one of Don Miguel Ruiz's Four Agreements, which I try to instill in her. But losing my cool is never okay, so I apologized the following day. I didn't make any excuses, and told her I was unpacking my feelings and reaction to the situation. We took the dog for a walk to the bus stop and talked. She's thirteen, so she doesn't always know how to articulate her feelings, but the important part is that I apologize when I do something wrong and then try again the next day.

There are plenty of times when I fall into lecture mode. I know I'm on the wrong track when my daughter answers with one-word responses. I try to give her space and ask open-ended questions. When I feel like she's overwhelmed or doesn't know what to say, I pull back and let her know I'm here when she's ready and wants to talk more. Then I check in with her later to see if she has questions or concerns she's ready to discuss. Once she starts asking questions, I know it will be a productive conversation.

I'm a work in progress. I'm not on a journey but a learning path. Some things take me longer to learn than I wish they did, but I'm learning nonetheless. Even slow forward progress is progress. I'm a big guy with a big personality, and I can be a little intimidating. My daughter is the opposite. She's sweet and kind and soft. She's wonderful—everything I wish I was. So I try to tread lightly and let her be herself while also having blunt conversations when necessary.

Doing the opposite of what my parents did and getting sober has allowed me to create the kind of family I always wanted. Family are my ride-or-die people, regardless of DNA. I wish my dad was still here to see how far I've come. I wish he could've stopped drinking and using. He was a troubled soul, and every day on this earth was a struggle for him. That kind of constant battle against your demons is not living. He never lived one day in his life. In a way, I live for both of us because he never got to. It's a bittersweet feeling. I'm sober, my company is growing, I get to share my story through this book, and I get to be present for my family, especially my daughter. Even my worst day today is better than any day my dad ever lived.

This year, I spent my birthday quietly with my favorite person, my daughter. Spending that day on my boat in the ocean in Florida with Ari was exactly what I wanted to do. This past year is the first year I've truly lived after struggling through my first two years of sobriety. It has everything to do with being present with the people I choose to call family.

Exploring my family of origin and its impact on my life has changed my perspective on true loyalty and how to create loyal bonds with people I love.

CHAPTER FIVE

LOYALTY

The screech of fire engines startled me out of my sleep. Our house was on fire, and my stepdad had been stabbed. It was utter chaos, and I had no idea what was happening as my mom, stepdad, sister, and I scrambled into the front yard, where we saw orange flames and smoke billowing against the night sky.

I didn't realize until much later that my mother had come home from the bar, wasted and pissed. She and my stepdad had different bedrooms by that point because their relationship was volatile and often violent. He'd reinforced his door with a slab of wood and a new handle and lock, so she couldn't get in while he was sleeping. In her drunken attempt to get to him in the bedroom, she lit an Aquanet hairspray bottle on fire and used it as a blow torch, eventually catching the door on fire. Once she smoked him out of his room, she stabbed him with a knife.

And you know what happened next? Nothing.

This was South Warren in the '80s. First, nobody gave a fuck about poor drunks and their kids. And second, my stepdad refused to rat out my mom. My stepdad and mom hated each other (or at least they acted like it). But when it came time to talk to anyone about what happened, my stepdad said it was just an accident. It sounds insane—because it is. And yet, that's the twisted sense of loyalty I grew up with. You don't snitch; no matter how dysfunctional and violent your family is, you will not tell anyone outside the family about it.

What I learned about misplaced loyalty from my mom and stepdad, is what kept me in that hellhole of a house. I never told my dad or grandparents about the real extent of the abuse I suffered. They didn't know how bad it was. I never took my sister's advice to call her social worker and get out of there. I didn't want to be disloyal. I was scared, and it was obvious that the adults all around me who could have helped or seen that something was going on (teachers, cops, firefighters, doctors, neighbors, and so on) were more comfortable if I just kept my mouth shut and pretended I was okay.

The friends who'd become my family were escaping similar home situations as mine. We got into a lot of fights. I'm not proud of it. I beat other people only because they'd messed with one of my buddies, and when that happened, all of us were expected to follow the code. You fuck with one of us, you fuck with all of us. More times than I can count, one of us would get jumped and immediately assemble all the others for payback. I thought this was family, love, and loyalty. Really, it was insanity—but it was all I had. Most of the guys I used to run with are dead or in jail now. They got stuck in their lives of drinking, drugs, violence, and poverty and never made it out of Warren.

In this chapter, I'll tell you about the false sense of loyalty I grew up with and how I slowly redefined what loyalty means in my current relationships.

LOYALTY ISN'T LOVE

Throughout my childhood, I mistook conditional loyalty for love. What I wanted was unconditional love from my parents. I never got it, so I settled for this transactional exchange of loyalties among my friends (we don't snitch on each other) that felt like love but wasn't. I thought the more I could prove to others how loyal I was, the more I would earn their loyalty in return. I was desperate for anything that felt like love and acceptance because I didn't love myself. I didn't realize until much later that my lack of self-love made me vulnerable to give loyalty to people who didn't deserve it or exploited it.

LOYALTY TO MY CHOSEN FAMILY

Attending Western Michigan University and being part of my fraternity initially seemed to show a lot of promise in the loyalty department. To be fair, my high school buddies had gotten into a massive fistfight with each other at my high school graduation, so my expectations of friendship and brotherhood were low.

Things were good with my fraternity brothers for a long time. I only realized much later that I tried way too hard to earn my frat brothers' loyalty.

We partied hard, but nobody ever got shot like at the parties back home. My grandparents lived a couple hours from college but centrally located to many of my buddies' childhood homes, so we often crashed at their house after a night of drinking and partying. I usually brought a couple of friends with me, but many times there were up to a dozen of us coming over in the middle of the night, raiding the fridge, then passing out all over the house. In the mornings, my grandpa would make home-made waffles with blueberries and hold the fresh waffles under our noses to wake us up. My grandpa wasn't exactly sweet and loving. All he knew to do was work and provide for his family, but getting up early and making breakfast from scratch for my hungover friends and me felt like loyalty and love.

The first time I got arrested for selling a pound of weed, nothing much happened. My grandparents stuck by me, and I only got a slap on the wrist. The second time, though, was a different story. A few of my frat brothers and I had a legit cocaine ring going. It was only a matter of time until we got busted. What I didn't expect, though, was that everyone involved would turn their backs on me and throw me under the bus. Most of them took plea deals and testified against me. My grandparents cut me off for a while but came back around when I made my case to them and they saw that I took responsibility.

That whole "snitches get stitches" bullshit on TV is not reality. I sold the drugs. I put my buddies in a situation where they had to choose themselves or loyalty to me. Of course, they chose themselves. When push comes to shove, 99 percent of people will cover their own ass.

Three of my frat brothers stood by me through the ordeal, and we're friends to this day. My grandparents continued to love and support me, and we stayed close until their deaths. Carrie, my girlfriend at the time, was incredibly loyal. She visited me twice a week, every week, while I was in jail. She was there for me when my father died. She was a good, kind person. I confused her loyalty with love and married her when I was twenty-four. I was young and stupid. I started my company, started making good money, started feeling like I had to let the world know I was big shit. She ultimately figured out that I'd been running around cheating on her. She asked for a divorce after about five years of marriage. She deserved better than what I could give her at the time. Twenty years later, I'd kill to find a woman like her. She's the one that got away, and last time I checked, she was happily married with kids. I'm glad for her and hope she knows that the loyalty and kindness I couldn't appreciate at twenty-four mean a lot to me now.

Sometimes we confuse loyalty with agreement. We may think our friends or family members are loyal to us if they agree with us and don't question our behaviors. But "yes" people aren't loyal, they're spineless. I value the few close friends and family members who always gave it to me straight and challenged me when I wanted to do something stupid. I want people to be loyal to me *and* my best interests, meaning they tell me what I need to hear, not what I want to hear.

Both my grandpa and grandma developed dementia and needed a lot of assistance in their final years. My grandpa eventually had to live in a nursing home when he required around-the-clock care. I visited him and we shared a scotch every other day. I'd start drinking again right now, if it meant I could have one more drink and conversation with him.

After three years in the nursing home, my grandpa died, and my grandma deteriorated so much that she had to enter the same nursing home. She died a couple of years later. During those nursing home visits, my grandparents told me stories from their childhood and adult years before I was born. They couldn't remember what happened the day before, but their memories from decades ago were as sharp as ever. I loved hearing those anecdotes, even the horrible stories about the Holocaust, because it made me feel closer to them. They had always asked me lots of questions and given me good advice, but it wasn't until dementia took over that they shared more vulnerable and personal stories with me.

While watching their decline was difficult, that time will always hold special significance for me. I was given the opportunity to show the same love and loyalty to the people who had extended them so generously to me. I chose my daughter Arianna's middle name, Rae, after my grandmother's first name. It's one meaningful way for me to honor my grandparents' loyalty to me. When they passed on, I was at their side when they took their last breaths, and gave the eulogy at both their funerals.

LOYALTY TO MYSELF

I can't force anyone to be loyal to me. I can't even prevent people from actively betraying me. It sucked being snitched on by my frat brothers when we were all selling drugs, not just me. It sucked being cheated on by my ex-fiancée over and over again. It sucked being dropped by friends, clients, and business partners once I stopped drinking.

I can't control anyone else, but I can be fiercely loyal to myself. I can stand up and advocate for myself and a second chance at an education and successful life after going to jail for selling drugs. I can walk away from a relationship that's not based on love, trust, and respect. I can cut ties with employees, friends, and business partners who are not aligned with my values. I've learned that loyalty doesn't mean letting people walk all over me. I no longer subscribe to my mom and stepdad's twisted sense of loyalty. Loyalty turns toxic once it requires me to abandon myself for someone else.

None of these decisions or conversations are easy, but being loyal to myself makes them necessary and possible. The same goes for smaller everyday habits that I know are good for me but difficult to follow through on every single day. If it's eighty degrees and sunny out, I know everyone and their grandmother are out drinking and partying while I sit in my office grinding, then making dinner for my daughter, and getting in some reading before an early bedtime so I can get up at the ass crack of dawn to crank out a lift. I feel about a million times better after quitting alcohol, but I still have bad days when I'm exhausted and just want to clear my calendar and do absolutely nothing. As the boss, I could easily do that. Sometimes being loyal to myself will mean taking a day off to rest or taking a twenty-minute nap. Sometimes it will mean telling myself to get my ass to the gym or call a friend for support. Sometimes it will mean powering through a meeting, and sometimes it will mean canceling that meeting.

The key to making these decisions with future me in mind while considering the needs of current me is loyalty to myself. What I do in each situation depends on the circumstances, my needs, and the needs of others involved. I do right by me and take care of myself, so I can be and do my very best for everyone around me.

LOYALTY IN BUSINESS

In January 2019, a week after I quit drinking, Dave, my COO, left NTM and eventually went to work for NTM's biggest client. I learned later that Dave had angled for a position with that client while instructing them on how to get out of their NTM contract. Dave had orchestrated all this behind my back while pretending we were friends, even family. I was on a first-name basis with his wife and kids. I attended family functions. I cared deeply about Dave.

I didn't understand why he would leave right when I got sober. I wondered if he somehow liked me better when I was drunk and unaware of what he was doing every day. Once I quit drinking, I became much more involved in the day-to-day business and took charge of the company. Maybe he just didn't want to be bothered. I'll never know.

After Dave left, and well into the pandemic, a colleague introduced me to Chrissy and we clicked. At the time, I had no money to hire another person, and no position she might fit. We share the same values, work ethic, and similar worldview. Chrissy is a wonderful, intelligent, kind person who's been sober for sixteen years and is deeply invested in her personal and professional growth. At around the same time, I decided to implement EOS, and my Director of Operations resigned. He saw that I was taking the company in a new direction and told me, *I got you here, but I can't get you there. It's time I move on.* Bam. Magically, the perfect position and revenue to pay Chrissy had opened up. She became my number two in the spring of 2021. Being loyal to myself and my business values and vision attracted the right person at the right time.

Chrissy is brilliant and is continually getting offers to work for other companies for more money. She keeps turning them down because she believes in what we're building together at NTM. It's a huge compliment to me, and I trust that we will do great things together because we're both self-aware and aligned with the company's mission. The irony isn't lost on me that I had to go through Dave's betrayal to get clarity on the kind of people I wanted to work with (and stay away from). I believe that experience allowed me to be open to Chrissy walking into NTM and igniting a powerful new partnership.

Chrissy is the integrator I need to implement EOS on a daily basis. She takes shit from nobody, and I'm in awe of her. She's an absolute badass, and nothing rattles her—except me. We fight like brother and sister, but we deeply respect each other and have each other's backs. That's true loyalty.

LOYALTY TO OUR CUSTOMERS

During the pandemic, we focused on getting our existing customers set up for success in our new remote work world. We see our current customers as our priority over acquiring new customers. I never understood why cell phone providers give better deals to new customers than existing ones. They only change their tune once you call to cancel—all of a sudden, they notice you're eligible for all kinds of deals! That's so backward. It's a lot like how the first-round draft pick in the NFL gets the biggest deal, instead of the team members that have already proven their value.

At NTM, we appreciate and reward loyal customers first. They've already put their trust in us, and our primary objective is to honor that trust by consistently overdelivering on our promises and ensuring they're getting the best deal. I take care of the people who take care of me. I'm proud that NTM has several clients who've been with us for nearly twenty years, and I will do my best to keep it that way.

Working out my complicated feelings and experiences with loyalty in childhood, personal relationships, and business dealings, helped usher in a new era in my life. Although I saw it as a breach of loyalty, my frat brothers snitching on me and taking plea deals to save their own asses set me on a path of growth I'm grateful for decades later.

Arianna and me at her bat mitzvah. Proud dad moment. She's beautiful.

Myself, Ari, and my sister Lesia. Breaking the cycle of abuse.

My sister Lesia and I, out enjoying life. Love her.

First cousins. Of course, I am extra!

One of the rare happy childhood moments of my sister and me.

My father Jeff, my hero at the time. He was wise beyond his addictions.

Food was a scarcity growing up. It is still a trigger for me today. Joyful moment eating at my grandparents'.

The day my "why" was born. Arianna came two weeks early and extremely tiny, four pounds and three ounces.

Dancing with my baby at my cousin's wedding.

Looking dapper with my dad at my uncle's wedding. I remember this day like it was yesterday even though it was forty years ago.

The one and only picture of my mother and father.

My father, Superman high on drugs but living life his way with his best friend.

Three generations of Siegels. My grandfather Edwin Siegel, my uncle Harry, and me. Wisdom and love.

Yet again, my uncle Harry doing his best to guide me with much appreciated knowledge. I believe this was my bachelor party.

My brother-in-law Ed, me, and my Uncle Harry. Everyone looking sharp.

Ed and Rae Siegel, my grandparents on my father's side. They provided for me when my parents couldn't. Grateful.

Girl power. Arianna Siegel, the result of my *Harder than Life* journey.

CHAPTER SIX

GROWTH

"You're looking at sixty years in prison, Kelly. Take the deal."

After getting busted for selling cocaine when I was a college student at Western Michigan University, I faced decades in prison. If you were a student at Western Michigan University in 1995 and 1996, you likely got your weed or cocaine from me and my crew. I was young and dumb, and started dealing drugs almost accidentally.

A big frat party was coming up, and someone asked me if I could get my hands on some blow. Back in Warren, everyone did coke, so I called up a buddy from elementary school who was a coke dealer and made an introduction. At the time, I didn't even do drugs; I just loved drinking. My old buddy walked into the frat house the day after the party and handed me $1,200. I thought I was just connecting supply and demand, but he gave me a cut for setting up the deal. I put the money in my pocket, thinking that was a lot of dough for doing nothing. Making that much money as a poor college student was just too tempting.

I knew I was guilty, but I was pissed, too, because I was taking the fall for everyone else who snitched on me. Some of my best friends turned on me. My fraternity kicked me out. My grandparents were deeply disappointed in me. The dean called me in to tell me I was suspended. "What about 'innocent until proven guilty'?" I tried to protest, but the dean wouldn't have it.

I knew I was guilty, but I also refused to let this setback derail my entire life. I didn't want to go back to South Warren. I had majorly fucked up, and I needed a second chance. I pleaded my case to the dean, asking what I would have to do to come back to school.

"Come back in a year with good grades from a community college, and I'll reinstate you."

When I faced serious prison time, I was defensive and angry at everyone—the police officers, my fraternity brothers, my grandparents, and the dean. Everyone. I took the plea deal. Fortunately, I would only end up serving four months of a one-year jail sentence. I participated in a work-release program that allowed me to take community college courses and work while serving my time. Walking into a jail cell for the first time and realizing my actions had taken away my freedom was both humbling and terrifying. I realized I had to take responsibility for my own actions, regardless of how I felt everyone else responded to the situation.

As promised, I came back to the university after a year. I had a 4.0 in my community college credits. When I walked across the stage at my graduation from Western Michigan University, the dean shook my hand: *I'm impressed. You had every opportunity to quit, but you didn't.*

I learned then that I could come back after making huge mistakes. I understood that I could grow back stronger. I'm glad I realized this when I was young because I had no idea about the growing pains I'd have to endure later in my life. No matter how tough it got, I was armed with the knowledge that I could leverage a growth mindset to overcome even the toughest obstacles and continue rebuilding myself and my life.

THE NIGHT IS DARKEST BEFORE THE DAWN

My life came crashing down around me in March 2020. In one day, my life was turned upside down along with the rest of the world: my company shut down, our biggest customer dropped NTM, and worst of all, I lost custody of my daughter, Arianna. March 20, 2020, is etched in most of our memories as the day the federal government shut down due to the pandemic. That morning I surrendered all passwords to my biggest client, as another vendor was taking over. I would later learn it was the client that Dave had gone to work for after abandoning NTM the year before. I was still reeling from that business loss, when I learned the entire country was shutting down, and I had to close the office.

However, I remember this day mostly for a phone call I received at 4:55 p.m. "Don't panic, Kelly," my lawyer told me calmly. My ex-wife and ex-fiancée had teamed up to convince a judge to take my daughter away. They lied and tried to paint me as an unfit parent, a violent person. I'd broken up with my ex-fiancée for good about two weeks earlier. I hadn't spoken to her, texted, or emailed her since; we'd had no communication whatsoever. But she still went to the police and filed a report about a fight we'd had more than a year before, accusing me of being violent and requesting a personal protective order. It had been a purely verbal altercation, but my ex-wife took that police report to family court and asked for full custody, saying I was a threat to our daughter.

At that point, I'd been sober for more than fourteen months, and no longer gave myself the option of numbing that betrayal with alcohol. I had to deal with that day's personal and financial losses and uncertainty fully conscious. I had no idea whether COVID would last two weeks or two years. I didn't know if courts would remain open, and for how long I wouldn't be able to see my daughter. I did know I could not stay away from her for long. If you told me today that I'd die if I went to see my daughter one more time, I'd be dead by tonight.

I had to sit with the fear, rage, and desperation as I stared into the abyss of a weekend that seemed like it stretched to eternity, before I could spring into action.

TOUGH TIMES DON'T LAST—BUT TOUGH PEOPLE DO

On Monday, my attorney introduced me to a family attorney, and we spent six hours hunkered down in her office, going over every detail, before she filed her brief with the court. I spent tens of thousands of dollars on this family attorney, but it was worth it because, in the end, I only had to go three days without my daughter. By Wednesday, I got to see and hug my beautiful girl again. In the end, the court agreed that my ex-wife and ex-fiancée had lied. I got more custody than before, had to pay less child support, and cleared my name. Most importantly, I got Ari back.

Although I've been in drunken fights with many dudes, I've

never hurt my ex-wife, ex-fiancée, or daughter. I've never been physically violent with any girl or woman in my entire life. My ex-fiancée has since apologized to me and is embarking on her own personal progress and sobriety journey. After the court ordeal, I met with my ex-wife and asked her three questions: *How can I be a better father? How can I be a better ex-husband? How can I be of service to you and your boyfriend?* Then I just listened and held space for everything that was on her mind, regardless of whether I thought it was valid. Hurt people hurt people, as the saying goes. Although I was betrayed and dragged through the mud by both women, I no longer felt that it was a personal attack on me or my parenting. I reframed it as an opportunity for self-growth. I could clearly see now that their behaviors were based on their own trauma and pain that had nothing to do with me. My ex-wife and I still disagree a lot, but our relationship has fundamentally changed. She knows I always have our daughter's best interests in mind.

EXTERNAL VS. INTERNAL GROWTH

I'll take sobriety over that Rolex on my wrist any day. When I was poor, growth meant cash and material goods—first food, then a car, clothes, jewelry, vacations, boats, and houses. Having grown up with drunk parents on welfare, growth meant starting my own business and raking in the dough. It's not like I'm a millionaire. I've made lots of money, and pissed most of it away. Aside from that insane Thailand trip, I've had $25,000 nights in Vegas and Miami, during which I wasted an embarrassing amount of money on excess booze and gambling. Even when I no longer had to worry about money, I always worried about money. I thought the outward markers of success would make me feel happy. They didn't. They had nothing to do with growth.

Accumulating stuff isn't growth. Don't get me wrong, I love nice stuff and overcompensate sometimes because I was poor for so long. I like buying things, and I like being generous and spoiling the people I care about. But I've come to realize that none of it matters as much as my internal growth.

I wear that Rose Gold Presidential Rolex with pride. Not as a status symbol, but as a reminder of a costly lesson I had to learn. I bought that Rolex for myself, when my ex-COO Dave left NTM shortly after I got sober. It signifies the lessons in loyalty I've learned and the emotional, mental, and professional growth that resulted from that painful situation. Yes, it's a flashy watch, but so what? All of my birthdays as a kid sucked, so I will absolutely buy gifts to remind myself that I'm valuable and to commemorate personal or business growth that deserves a reward in my eyes. Don't let other people tell you how to spend your own money.

Sobriety opened the door to personal and professional growth and development I could never have imagined. Instead of drinking for temporary relief on March 20, 2020, I stayed present. That challenging situation took everything out of me but also led me on a path of growth. I sought out hypnotherapy to work through my mom and stepdad's abuse and neglect. I doubled down on my sobriety and personal progress. I bought a home gym so I could continue working out through the pandemic. I started meditating and journaling. I restructured my entire business. I started writing this book. And most importantly, I grew even closer to my daughter. She'll never forget how I fought to get her back and how much I love her.

GROWTH AT WORK

When it comes to my work family, it's important to me to create the best possible circumstances for growth for everyone. It makes me happy to see employees get married, buy houses, get advanced degrees and certifications, and have kids graduate from high school and college. NTM pays 100 percent of employee health insurance—the good kind, not garbage insurance where you can't pick the doc you like, and nothing is covered. We provide 401(k) matching and continuing education and strive to double our revenue, so we can offer the highest salaries in the industry. I believe giving people the financial security to focus on personal and professional growth is essential.

Growing NTM has been my sole focus since I quit drinking. Although we've been in business for several decades, we've overhauled the company completely in the past few years. It feels like a startup again, all shiny and new, because my sober self has bigger goals and a more ambitious vision than my drunk self did. As it turns out, the same pandemic that folded many companies contributed to NTM's growth and restructuring. Because our IT services were deemed essential, we were not required to fully shut down. We had a discussion as a team and gave employees the option to work from the office or from home. We supported one employee who was high risk and elected to work remotely. The rest of us stayed in the office. We set up all our clients for remote work so their companies could continue to function.

Losing our biggest client right when the pandemic shut everything down turned out to be a blessing in disguise. Because we'd lost such a significant portion of our revenue, we met the eligibility requirements for the Paycheck Protection Program

(PPP) loans. We used the PPP money to keep everyone on the team employed, and it bought us some breathing room to figure out our next steps.

Most of our clients were working remotely over the summer, so we decided it was the perfect time to standardize everyone's office hardware, replace outdated machines and devices, fix any issues that could cause downtime in the future, and set all our clients up for success once they returned to their offices. This huge effort was much easier to achieve with everyone working remotely and our NTM team having access to empty offices. We did our work undisturbed and without compromising our clients' efficiency.

EOS—THE ENTREPRENEURIAL OPERATING SYSTEM

Implementing EOS has been a vital tool to set NTM up for meteoric growth. We've envisioned our one-year, three-year, and ten-year goals, and mapped out how to get there. We use a weekly scorecard to measure Key Performance Indicators (KPIs), such as support tickets solved, technician engagement on tickets, customer feedback, proposals, and closed deals. In short, we measure everything related to driving revenue, employee performance, and customer satisfaction.

Since implementing EOS, we've seen a 300 percent increase in customer feedback, with 95 percent of that feedback being positive. It shows that we've grown in our ability to engage our customers in a discussion on their experience with NTM, and of course, that their experiences are overwhelmingly positive.

GROWTH COMES FROM BEING WRONG

I listen to a lot of podcasts and am a voracious reader. I considered sharing a list of people I enjoy learning from but decided against it. I don't want you to pick people based on my recommendations, and I know I would inadvertently leave out someone who's taught me a lot. I will say this: I listen to progressives and conservatives, Christian, Jewish, Muslim, and atheist voices. I take what I like and leave the rest. I don't put anyone on a pedestal and have no problem with the fact that everyone will say and do stupid things. That doesn't destroy everything good they've ever said or done, but it also keeps me from pretending there are any gurus out there who are infallible and perfect.

I pay attention to how what I consume makes me feel. Maybe someone I used to enjoy listening to is going down the conspiracy theory rabbit hole, skewing too religious or too woke, or spewing rants rather than providing thoughtful content. My growth is my own, and while I am open to learning from others, I know my path is specific to me, and I must do the hard inner work myself, instead of following someone else's template.

I try to avoid extremes and living in echo chambers on social media. I purposely seek out people I disagree with and learn from a wide variety of thinkers because I believe in constantly challenging myself. What's the point in only listening to or talking with people who already agree with me? I'm here to learn, not to get my ego stroked. I don't care about tribalism and putting people in boxes. I don't ascribe to a party or religion because I want to be seen as an individual and see others as individuals.

"I was wrong once, but I was mistaken." It's a joke—but not really. I actually lived by that statement for a long time, until I realized that true growth only comes from allowing the possibility of being wrong, even inviting and embracing it. I constantly question, "Where could I be wrong on this?" and I often realize that I am or that there are at least many other valid ways to look at a situation. I love spirited discussions with people who view things differently because it opens my eyes to other possibilities. I'm wrong a lot. I don't have all the answers. That's not shameful, it's liberating! It's the only way to learn and grow.

WORK IN PROGRESS

It's a cliché because it's true. I'll never stop growing, which is sometimes an uncomfortable place to be. I feel a sense of urgency because I've wasted a lot of time being drunk, but growth can't be rushed. There are certain days when I'm totally overwhelmed with how far I still have to go, how much childhood trauma I still have to process, and how many business goals I still want to reach, and I wonder if I'll ever get there. But then I remind myself that all I need to do is stay committed to working on myself. It's a never-ending process that will only stop once I stop breathing.

Work works. There is no way to work as hard as I do and not see growth. And, of course, the harder I work, the luckier I get. This growth mindset impacts every facet of my personal and professional life, especially my physical, emotional, and mental health.

CHAPTER SEVEN

HEALTH

I was at work when I received the call I'd been dreading. I knew it was coming, but nothing could have prepared me. "We just admitted your father to the ER. He's unresponsive." I calmly responded that I would be right there, told my boss I had a family matter to deal with, then walked out of the office and burst into tears. I knew this was the end for my dad. He would never regain consciousness.

Two days later, in the early morning hours, I was with my dad when he took his last labored breath. As I walked out of the hospital, all I could think about was how I wanted to get wasted, but all the bars were closed. So, instead, I walked up to my brand-new truck and punched a giant dent in its side. The punch was not for my dad's death, but for what could have been, for the life he could have lived but didn't. The man he could have been but wasn't.

Alcohol and heroin killed my dad on Mother's Day, 1999; he was only forty-six years old. I was twenty-three. My idea of grieving was going on a bender that lasted all summer until Labor Day. I didn't experience a single sober day throughout that nearly four-month period.

I had an extremely high tolerance, but those few months were rough even on me. The level of excess and recklessness I exhibited matched the pain and grief I felt over my father's death. After I quit drinking, a friend joked with me that everyone is allotted so many alcoholic beverages in their life, and I had drunk all of mine already.

I learned later that my uncle was so concerned about me that he was planning an intervention. That would not have gone over well, since I will not be told what to do. However, the Tuesday after Labor Day, I flipped a switch and decided to scale my drinking way back. I remember it as the first glimmer of being sick and tired of being sick and tired. I was tired of escaping, numbing, running away, and not living up to my potential. I didn't quit alcohol completely, and it would be decades until I would, but it was the first time I got the feeling there had to be a better way, a better life.

I didn't want to end up like my dad. I didn't want to waste my life. So while I wasn't yet ready to deal with my main crutch for coping with my childhood trauma, I did start paying more attention to my health and making changes to my habits and routine that I've maintained to this day. Since I finally quit alcohol, I've added more, especially when it comes to my mental and emotional health. Up to that point, I'd been primarily focused on my physical health and fitness. Yeah, I know; it's a bit hypocritical. I looked like I was in good physical shape for most of my life, while guzzling poison every day—but you have to start somewhere.

This chapter discusses what has worked for me, but it's not advice for you. I hope you'll use it more as inspiration to find your own path. I'm not interested in receiving unsolicited advice, so I try not to give it. I'm always surprised by how many people in shitty relationships dole out dating advice. I live my life and share what I do in case other people want to know. Aside from that, I keep my mouth shut. There is no one right way, and what works for me might not work for you. But, however you decide to navigate your path to better health, why not make the first step today?

CUSTOMIZE YOUR HEALTH ROUTINE

There are many resources about structuring your day, creating a morning routine, learning mindfulness, and more. I'll share what has worked for me in dealing with the anger and loneliness underlying my desire to drink and do drugs. I'll tell you what I do to keep myself physically and mentally healthy. Take what you like and leave the rest. There is no magic bullet and no one-size-fits-all approach. I have a lot of go-to's, and I mix and match them as needed. So can you. Don't take my routine as a specific schedule to emulate, but rather as inspiration to try out lots of different things and see what works for you.

EXERCISE

I get up at 4:30 a.m. every morning to work out. Remember I told you how scrawny I was growing up? I worked my ass off for decades at the gym to bulk up, and continue to do it every single day.

Initially, I started lifting weights because my home was filled with violence. My mom and stepdad beat the shit out of me, and I was physically outmatched. I worked out to get bigger, so I could feel safer and survive. And, yeah, so that I could punch my stepdad in the face if necessary. It never came to that because he only felt strong in front of a little boy, but had nothing to say to me once I moved out. I was itching for a confrontation, and he knew it. But by that point, it wouldn't have felt right to punch an old man, so I just walked away and never looked back.

While it was a survival strategy early on to protect myself against my stepdad and mom's vicious beatings, physical exercise has gone on to become one of my constants, a great stress relief, and a daily habit that keeps my mind clear and focused and gives me a sense of accomplishment early in the day. I usually listen to a self-development or business podcast while I'm working out, instead of music. My time is limited, and I love getting a dose of motivation, inspiration, or a new idea to implement personally or professionally.

I don't half-ass my workouts, and I mix them up frequently. Changing my exercise routine prevents me from phoning it in and provides the challenge I need to stave off boredom. I even have several gym memberships, in addition to a home gym, so that I can alternate where I work out and learn the best routines and exercises from a variety of different sources. If I'm staring at you at the gym, it's probably because you're doing an exercise I've either forgotten about or never tried, and I'm intrigued. I have a student mindset, always. After thirty years, I still learn a new exercise almost every week.

I hit the gym every day unless I'm going to play golf—sore muscles and golf don't mix. Because I'm so big, I have the ugliest golf swing you've ever seen. Straight, no backswing. My friends always crack up and take videos of me because nobody can figure out how I even hit the ball with that technique.

If you're not into the gym and lifting and hate golf, there are a million other options you can choose from. Don't have money for a gym membership? I call bullshit because you can get them for $15/month these days. But if you really can't afford that, go for a run! Can't run because of your joints? Go for a bike ride or swim at the local community pool. Make it something you like doing, and that gives you a good sweat and gets some endorphins pumping. I love weightlifting because of its multiple health benefits, such as improved cardiovascular strength, stronger bones, better mood, and increased energy. However, if strength training is not your thing, do something else. You don't have to go for hour-long sessions seven days a week like me; shoot for three forty-five-minute sessions a week.

You have no excuse. Go move your body. Your heart will thank you. Your mind will thank you. Your family will thank you.

PUSH YOURSELF, BUT DON'T KILL YOURSELF

This should be obvious, but it's not. It's very tempting to either take it too easy or go so hard that you'll hurt yourself. It takes practice to walk the line between getting a really great workout and not jeopardizing your health. I'm in my mid-forties now, so I'm not repping 400 pounds anymore. I go with 245 pounds instead, knowing that I'll still get a killer workout, without risking a serious injury. That doesn't mean you should do the same. Work with a trainer, take a class, and go slow. Don't compare yourself to others or try to match me if you've never lifted. I've worked up to this over decades. I'm all for scorching earth in the gym, but don't be a dumbass. I've seen guys try to prove something and end up tearing their biceps or ripping their ACL as a result. What good does that do? My daughter and my work family depend on me, so I try not to be an idiot.

Of course, it took me a while to learn all of this myself. Back in college, I wanted to level up my game and started hanging out with Gus and Damien, two buddies who just happened to be bodybuilders. These gigantic goons were great guys, but they absolutely destroyed me in the gym. They were 6'2" and 6'3" respectively, 260 pounds, and absolutely massive. Gus's party trick was eating lit cigarettes. You wouldn't want to fuck with either of them, but in the gym, they turned into my personal cheerleaders. *Hey Kelly,* they'd say, *we don't have the time to take these weights off, so you're just gonna lift the same as us. Cool?* Not cool. I thought my arms were going to rip off, doing skull crushers during that first workout. I was deceptively strong, but these dudes pushed me right to the brink. This was nearly thirty years ago, and I can still see their faces hovering over me, yelling: *Yeah, man! Big arms! Big chest!* In other words, there is a time to be stupid and reckless and risk ripping every muscle in your body, and there is a time to grow up and make sure you live another day to pay the bills and be a functioning parent to your kid.

Take your age and circumstances into consideration when it comes to working out. I've been 220 pounds since college, but I've looked very different depending on my life stage. When I first started working out seriously, I saw the most significant muscle gains, and it was really exciting to transform myself from a scrawny kid into a big guy with an imposing stature. My ex-wife had a really rough pregnancy, so I spent a lot of time taking care of her and didn't get to the gym as much during those months. I lost muscle and gained fat and hated how I looked. After Arianna was born, I went back to the gym to cut and recomp, but I never forgot that time. I don't ever want to be scrawny or fat again. I like the way I look, which is an incentive to keep chiseling that rock, even if my fifty-inch chest requires custom suits. The older I get, the more muscle atrophy I have to deal with. It sucks, but I deal with reality. My goal isn't to get bigger but to get better. I don't want to add more muscle to my frame. I want to define the existing muscle. When you look good, you feel good, and then you do good. So for me, a good day always begins with a workout.

I don't believe in maintenance regimens. You're either growing or dying. Age and circumstance make it so the gains aren't as significant as they once were, and they come slower and more incrementally, but I prefer that over stagnation.

Exercise is a daily constant in my life, but for the rest of my morning routine, I mix and match whatever I feel I need the most that day. Most often, I add a quick meditation, gratitude practice, and breakfast with my daughter. I think it's essential to be flexible with your morning routine and add and subtract aspects as needed. And if you're not a morning person, create a lunch or bedtime routine. The important part is to make time in your day for the habits that support your physical, emotional, and mental health.

MEDITATION

An old Zen proverb goes something like this: "If you don't have time to meditate for an hour every day, you should meditate for two hours." Some variations of the quote refer to thirty minutes or an hour, but the point is clear: meditation is precisely for the times when we feel too busy, too overwhelmed, or too stressed to practice stillness and focus.

After my workout, I meditate. I used to hate meditating. Okay, I still do. I've been doing it for years, and I suck at it. It's still hard for me because my brain goes a million miles a minute. But the few times I've achieved a moment of mental peace and clarity are worth it, so I'll keep practicing.

Some of the resources I use are the Calm meditation app, specifically the "Daily Calm" and the "Daily Jay" meditations. These short meditations are a good starting point for a meditation hater like me. Although I don't like meditating, I notice when I miss a day. I also find it valuable in moments of panic, like when I'm flying on a plane. I use a short meditation by author and motivational speaker Mel Robbins (*I'm loved, I'm safe, I'm okay*) and repeat it a million times like a mantra.

I've read all of Joe Dispenza's books on meditation, which are pretty complex and challenging to understand. My biggest takeaway is to be no one, no thing, and no place. In other words, be free of ego. Being here and now and giving my brain a break to rest. I'm a total amateur at meditating, but that doesn't matter.

Then I get ready and high-five myself in the mirror (thanks, Mel Robbins!). Every day I have breakfast with my daughter. Those few minutes before our separate days start are an important touch-in point and are non-negotiable for me. I take her to school every day, and then head to work. At some point during the day, I try to nap (either in my chair or in my car). My overall quality of sleep is terrible, and it's something I'm still trying to figure out. Nobody has all the parts in place, but sleep is hugely important, so until I can figure out how to sleep better at night, I'm going to do what I can and take a nap to give me a second wind for the rest of the day.

After work, I have dinner with my daughter, do a quick gratitude journal practice, and spend evenings reading or with friends. I'm not a fan of TV and screens, in general. I prefer books and podcasts that teach me something or spending face-to-face time with people I love.

SLEEP

I wish I'd hacked sleeping by now, but I haven't. I've seen doctors about my insomnia, tried supplements, meditation, and nightly sleep routines—nothing has worked! I still wake up a million times throughout the night, having to pee or ruminating over a work problem and unable to go back to sleep. Because I don't sleep well, I slam caffeine all day, which makes sleep harder the next night. It's a vicious cycle I haven't been able to escape yet.

My doc did all the tests, and everything came back fine, so he handed me some sleeping pills. That's always the answer, isn't it? Pills. I took them a few times when I absolutely couldn't sleep at all, but they make me wake up groggy and still tired. I stopped taking them and am back at square one.

It's incredibly frustrating, but I told you that I would give it to you straight. I don't have everything figured out yet, and anyone pretending to is lying to you. No matter how much progress I make, I know there will always be aspects of my life that require more attention and improvements. For me right now, that's sleep. It may be something else for you—perhaps nutrition, exercise, or mental health. Don't beat yourself up. All you can do is take the small steps toward improvement, remain open to new information, and be willing to experiment and deploy patience. Health is not about perfection but about making as many positive choices every day as possible.

FOOD

People think I eat clean because of how I look. I don't. I don't eat cigarettes like Gus, but I desperately need more veggies, especially greens, in my life. I have pretty consistent stomach problems, and my doc keeps telling me that I need more fiber and more greens in my diet. I'm telling you because I hate those personal development books where the author makes it sound like every part of their routine is perfect. Food is nutrition, but it's also survival, security, comfort, and family for me.

Growing up, we got welfare cheese, powdered milk, and tomato soup. I'm grateful for that food as it was the only thing in the fridge and cabinet most days, but if you served me tomato soup today, I would likely throw it across the room. While those cheese blocks kept me alive, they will always remind me of the cold, lonely, neglectful house I grew up in. As I said in a previous chapter, I started my paper route to buy food, not comic books. Good food is a comfort to me, and sharing a meal with loved ones and friends or hosting a cookout is one of my very favorite things to do. The best get-togethers are spontaneous barbecues with a horde of friends and family, throwing some cut-up chicken in a marinade, and wrapping a pile of ears of sweet corn in aluminum foil. A simple, healthy meal that's off-the-charts delicious straight from the grill. I love feeding people almost as much as I love eating. My grandparents instilled this appreciation for regular meals paired with good company and good conversation in me when I was in college and ate a meal with them every single day.

I don't hide my love for food or why it's so important to me. I recently had a great conversation with a potential business partner over a delicious meal. We talked about our shared appreciation for good food. I don't take food lightly because, no matter how much I've worked on my childhood trauma, I'm still that kid who didn't have anything in the fridge to eat. I secretly still feel like I'm one bad break away from having to eat tomato soup again. So, when I go out and eat a big, beautiful steak at an expensive restaurant, I acknowledge my gratitude for getting to enjoy this tasty meal that I worked really hard for.

Although I love a fancy dinner, deep down, I'm a meat and potatoes kind of guy, and that likely won't change. I try to eat real food, rather than processed snacks and fast food, but sometimes it's unavoidable, especially on busy days. I keep protein bars and shakes within arm's reach at all times. I'm hungry 24/7 and eat four to six times a day. I have breakfast around 7:00 a.m. with my daughter, lunch at noon, and dinner at 6:00 p.m. Depending on my plans for the night, I eat a snack at 10:00 a.m., 2:00 p.m., and sometime after dinner. I try to have all my meals sitting down at a table, with my daughter, friends, or extended family.

My daughter loves to bake. I'll eat anything chocolate she makes, but lemon Jolly Ranchers and carrot cake are my kryptonite. My

Grandma Siegel always had a big jar of hard candies—but not Jolly Ranchers. They didn't pay top dollar for fancy brand-name candy. She had the store brand knock-off, but that wasn't the point. She made my life a little sweeter by putting out the jar of candies or sending little care packages with me to college. Sweets remind me of my grandparents' house, of being fed and loved and safe. Naturally, sweets are the way to my heart. I've always had a sweet tooth, but especially since I quit drinking. Alcohol converts to sugar in the body, so getting sober ratcheted up my cravings to get sugar in a different form. When I go out for dinner, I always get dessert. It's non-negotiable.

Aside from my sweet tooth and lack of leafy greens, I eat mostly healthy food. I stay away from fried foods. Yeah, I know, boring, but effective. Nutrition, exercise, sleep, and stress management are essential to good health and, therefore, self-awareness and presence. We all know it, yet people want to believe that taking a new supplement, trying ice-cold showers, or learning from that one guru will be the ticket. For me, the tried-and-true everyday habits do the heavy lifting. Of course, any shiny new tools may become a part of your routine, but I would focus on nailing down the basics first.

At the same time, I don't advocate being super rigid. I've certainly seen a difference in my energy levels and physique when I've cut out sugar and caffeine, and if that's your jam, go for it. I've tried to moderate my sugar and caffeine intake for a few weeks or months at a time. It's difficult because I rely so much on caffeine on the days that I've slept badly. I've seen a difference in my joints when cutting caffeine and alcohol, which I believe came from not being so insanely dehydrated from too much coffee and booze anymore. However, I still rely on caffeine and enjoy sugar way too much to give it up completely. Moderation and balance in all aspects is key.

THERAPY

I've worked with a therapist and several different coaches throughout my life because I take my emotional and mental health as seriously as my physical health. As the saying goes, "feeling is healing," and working through my emotions has finally freed me from the anger and resentment of my past. Being harder than life doesn't mean I have no feelings, and repressing the ugly shit will only take me right back to my crutches and masks. I'm done with that for good.

Therapy is not silly or weak or only for women. If you still think that way, I'll invite you to join us in this century. Emotional suppression is what most boys and men are taught from childhood, so I know how hard it is to break that cycle, but you absolutely must. If you don't take care of your insides, it doesn't matter how well you take care of your outside, because you will not be happy and peaceful.

Aside from my therapist, I've also worked with an emotional coach to hone my emotional intelligence and deal with some specific childhood trauma and unhealthy communication tactics. I came to her with specific issues that she helped me resolve. Therapy and coaching don't have to be long-term commitments. Sometimes years are necessary, and sometimes you can resolve issues in weeks or months. Sometimes, you'll need therapy more frequently, and sometimes a check-in every few weeks will do, depending on your needs. I've seen the same therapist for a dozen years, and now I see him once a month.

There may come a time when I'll meet weekly again, or I may stop altogether. The point is that therapy should be a flexible, fluid component of life.

During the pandemic, I tried twenty sessions of hypnotherapy. It was incredible. I went twice a week because I was trying to process the lack of love and care I received from my parents. In the third session, the therapist helped me release "the weight of the parents," and something broke loose inside of me. It felt like a physical burden lifting off my shoulders. I'm not saying it will work for you, only that it's important to consider all your options without dismissing them outright.

Currently, psychedelics are all the rage—MDMA, toad venom, psilocybin, and ayahuasca. I haven't tried them, and I'm not sure if I will. But if I do, I won't be the guy microdosing every day. I'll be the one in the jungle puking his guts out. Microdosing or smoking weed regularly just sounds too much like having a drink every day to take the edge off. I can understand some people using psychedelics in a controlled setting to achieve an emotional, mental, or spiritual breakthrough. To me, that's the difference. You can use it as a crutch, a mask, an escape in your daily life, or as a catalyst to break open a deep wound that needs healing. Are you using drugs or plant medicine? Are you using it to run away or to face yourself? I'd rather purge it all in one night and come back a better man than try microdosing. Just rip off the Band-Aid! Don't peel it slowly. I'd rather experience an intense but short-lived pain than an eternity of paper cuts.

I'm scared shitless of these ayahuasca sessions, but usually, that means I'll have to lean into that fear. Maybe my next book will be about my trip to Costa Rica to see what all the fuss is about.

MAKE THAT DAMN DOCTOR'S APPOINTMENT

I know you don't want to, but you definitely should. Especially men have a strange mental block when it comes to accessing medical care. Some of it is ego and the belief that we should just tough it out and suck it up. But, personally, I think it's more about fear and not wanting to face what we might find out. We pretend that we're invincible, but know that we're not. So, as long as we don't go to the doctor and don't find out the potentially horrible thing that could be wrong with us, it's not real. And finally, we don't want to change. We don't want to hear the doc say what we already know. *Hey, you've got high blood pressure and diabetes. You gotta lay off the bon-bons.* We don't want anyone to tell us to quit smoking or drinking, start exercising, lose weight, eat more fiber, and drink more water. We want to do whatever we feel like, no matter how bad it is for our health, without concerning ourselves with the likely consequences. And that's how fifty-year-olds drop dead from cardiac arrest one day: because they never cared to go to the doc and figure out their irregular heartbeat.

I've bullshitted myself long enough. If I pay for excellent health care for my employees and want them to take care of their physical, emotional, and mental health, I must set the example. I believe in proactive, preventive care, rather than reactive, emergency care. I get regular check-ups, access medical treatment when I'm sick instead of "sucking it up," and go to therapy for my mental health. I've had everything checked, from my blood and my gut microbiome to my heart. I'm definitely procrastinating on the prostate exam and the colonoscopy...but I'll get there.

KNOW WHEN TO CUT YOURSELF SOME SLACK

When I was drinking, I ignored my body's signals. I'd get wasted, then punish myself with a grueling workout. I was all about playing hard and working harder. But that's not really what it means to take care of my health. Of course, pushing myself during a workout is vital, but it's more important to truly listen to what I need. I'm also practicing turning off my phone to create quiet times when I'm unavailable for social interactions or work messages. I allow myself to relax and veg out on the couch, watching movies, and yeah, eating a cupcake if I damn well please. It all comes back to self-awareness. I tend to be extreme, if you haven't noticed, so my focus is balance. I skew toward overworking, so making time for rest is an uncomfortable but essential practice for me.

PERFECTIONISM SETS YOU UP FOR FAILURE

When I have a shit day, I remind myself that it's just one day, or one meeting, or one workout. If I have a difficult day at work, that doesn't mean I "deserve" a drink at night to take the edge off. There is no point in ruminating over the bad day to the point where I stay up all night and start off the next day as badly as I ended the one before. Too often, one bad interaction or experience snowballs into the next, and before you know it, you've skipped your workout, yelled at your kid, and are sitting in the parking lot crying while stuffing donuts in your face. There are no perfect streaks, so these bumps in the road are to be expected. They're not an excuse to fall off the wagon entirely.

As I write this book, I'm the same age my dad was when he died. I don't know why some people are able to quit drinking, and some aren't. I still wish my dad could have turned it around. I felt like he never truly lived, so I had to live for both of us. In some way, I hope he can look down on me and live vicariously through me. At every milestone or exciting event, I think of my father. Arianna's birth, building a business, buying a house, meeting a woman, publishing this book—my dad is always right there with me.

My health is so important to me because I've wasted so many years being drunk that I need to keep myself in shape physically and mentally so I can accomplish everything I want to, and squeeze every last drop out of the time I've been given. Dementia runs in my family, so I fully expect to spend the last few years of my life not knowing who the hell I am. You can be damn sure I'll do everything in my power to extend the good years before I get to that point. Whatever your specific personal reasons are for wanting to make healthy changes, milk them as much as you can. This is your inspiration—the motivation that carries you through making the hard choices.

Being in the best physical, emotional, and mental health of my life is helping me double down on being tenacious.

CHAPTER EIGHT

TENACITY

When I was nine years old, my stepdad tried to kill me.

"Kelly, why is there water in the fucking bathtub?" my stepdad hissed through his teeth, his face contorted in rage, as he walked out of the bathroom. He'd come home wasted as usual, but my mom was still at the bar. My sister had moved out by this point. Still scrawny, I stared at my stepdad's giant frame, terror coursing through my body. I never knew which drunk I'd get walking through the door. Happy drunk, unconscious drunk, or angry drunk were all options in this twisted game of Russian roulette. That day, I got angry drunk.

While I was still stammering about my mom taking a bath before going to the bar, he grabbed me and dragged me into the bathroom. He yelled about how I should have let the water out before forcing my head into the tub and underwater. Nobody else was home. As my stepdad was drowning me, I thought, "This is it. I'm dead." Flailing my arms in the water and trying desperately to come up for air, my hand caught the drain plug, and at the last moment, I pulled the chain.

Shortly after that incident, I was home alone again when my stepdad came back from the bar. This time I got lucky. He was in a good mood. He handed me my first beer and sat down. Looking back, I understand how messed up it was that I was a fourth grader when I was introduced to alcohol by a parent. But then again, the asshole tried to kill me. However, in the moment, it almost felt like love, and it definitely felt like safety. There was a sweet spot when my stepdad was just buzzed enough to be happy (compared to his usual miserable self), but not so wasted that he got angry and cruel. I was starving for care and attention, and sharing this moment with my stepdad made me feel both grown up and equal to him. I felt safe because if we were drinking together and bullshitting like pals, he wouldn't rage at me and beat me.

At nine years old, in a split second, I learned that drinking meant connection and safety. I liked the feeling of being buzzed and thinking, *Whoa, this ain't so bad. I'm numb. He's happy*.

Sometimes I played records for my stepdad, he sang along, and we danced together. It was fun. But mostly, it was survival. I thought, *Okay, if I drink with him, he won't fucking kill me. He won't beat me. He won't drown me.* I always hoped it would last, but it never did. Every day we played Russian roulette again and again, and sometimes, if I was lucky, we landed on the illusion of connection.

I didn't come this far to only come this far. Over the years, I have built up a stockpile of grit, perseverance, and tenacity. According to Oxford Languages, *tenacity* is defined as:

- "the quality or fact of being very determined; determination"
- "the quality or fact of continuing to exist; persistence"

For most of my life, tenacity meant survival—the sheer determination to continue existing against all odds. Subconsciously I thought that if I stopped struggling, grinding, hustling, and pushing 24/7, I wouldn't just stop—I might actually die. It's only been in the last couple of years that I've been practicing being comfortable with patience, stillness, rest, and surrender. It feels totally contrary to my default setting and personality, but I know it's the path forward from surviving to thriving.

This will sound totally hippie, woo-woo, but stick with me here: I do talk to little Kelly, that scared, scrawny boy who didn't think he was worthy of love and attention. After that horrible imaginary conversation I had with my mom and stepdad during the counseling session I discussed in a previous chapter, I totally believe in taking care of our inner child. I actually hug myself and tell myself that I'm safe and loved. It sounds crazy. It *feels* crazy sometimes. But it works. I'm grateful for the tenacity that helped me survive. I'm even thankful for the hard motherfucker it made me. And I'm also grateful that in the life I've built, I can take off that armor, break down the walls, and stop constantly looking over my shoulder.

FROM SURVIVING TO THRIVING

Just like I started drinking to survive my stepdad, I kept drinking to survive relationships, social situations, and work. I figured other people would like me better if I drank with them, just like my stepdad. I enjoyed the buzz and the camaraderie, and the feeling of safety. As long as we were drinking together, we were having fun, and I wasn't in danger. Of course, drinking and drugs put me in a lot of terribly dangerous situations, but at my core, my childhood experiences were overriding any logic about the dangers of alcohol and drugs. I thought drinking helped me survive my childhood. Drinking meant survival, and survival meant tenacity. It took going really deep while writing this book to figure out that I used alcohol first as an actual survival mechanism and then kept doing it because, in a twisted way, it seemed to be working.

TENACITY THROUGH BUSINESS UPS AND DOWNS

When it comes to the business I chose—cyber security—my newfound self-awareness helped me realize that I picked it, in part, because I'm used to dealing with chaos and danger. It feels comfortable and familiar. The IT industry is fast-paced and constantly changing. Cyber security is under relentless attacks from hackers. If we do our work correctly, our customers will never know all the near misses and almost fatal strikes. Being in charge of keeping our customers safe is both thrilling and anxiety-producing for me. It requires the same grift and tenacity I drew from to make it through my childhood.

When I was still drinking, that anxiety often got the best of me, and I was harsh to my employees or acted erratically, taking days off at a time when I was hungover or wanted to party. Once I quit drinking, I realized what I'd put my work family through. Many of them stuck it out with me and showed a lot of tenacity of their own in the process. I've had the opportunity to mend many of these relationships, and we've grown together. Now I attract like-minded people who are self-aware and growth-minded like me.

TENACITY NEVER STOPS

So many people are self-medicating with alcohol, cannabis, prescription drugs, sex, or gambling. It's rare to be the buffalo walking through a shit storm, but that's what I do. I'm not going to repeat the same dysfunctional patterns I've seen my family and friends model. I lead by example. I walk the walk. I can say with 110 percent conviction that I am what I say I am. I live congruently, without a single skeleton in my basement. I'm not hiding a secret porn addiction or sneaking drinks. My old buddies might say I'm boring now, but I'm winning. I quit drinking to be a leader. I'm blissfully dissatisfied, meaning I'm happy with my progress, but I'll keep pushing because if you stop trying, you're dying. Tenacity never stops. Working on my business and implementing EOS, being a present father, writing a book, and publishing a podcast is all a lot of work! At the same time, I'm having fun with it. Otherwise, what's the point? I can be both: a bad motherfucker ready to scorch earth and a servant leader focused on helping as many people as possible.

I've been in therapy for years and will continue, probably as long as I live. Even if you can't go to therapy right now for whatever reason, if nothing else, let those feelings flow through your body and dissipate. It's pushing down those feelings, repressing them, that gives them power. Instead of using the energy it takes to keep them locked inside of you, let them out. Write down your feelings about your family. Notice your reactions to day-to-day things, positive and negative, and write them down. The difficult, negative emotions are signposts for the childhood trauma you need to investigate. If you can access therapy, do it. Be vulnerable and get that shit out of you so you can live your life. Just like me, you came too far to only come this far.

Tenacity has been one of the most important values in my life to get me to where I am today. My relentless determination has gotten me results I could only dream of.

CHAPTER NINE

RESULTS

I was crouched underneath a client's desk terminating a cable, when I heard the client talk about passing a message on to my "boss." To the client's surprise, I popped up.

Kelly? What are you doing here under my desk? he asked.

I explained to him that we were behind, so it was all hands on deck.

Of course, any entrepreneur needs to spend most of their time leading the company and creating strategy, but I'm right there in the trenches when stuff needs to get done. I'm not above manual labor. I'm not above menial tasks. And I don't hire anyone who thinks they are. I mean, what could be worse than dumping out piss jars? Certainly not installing hardware, even if it requires my giant frame to crumple up underneath office furniture. Nothing is below me when it comes to getting results for my company. I would empty a fucking piss jar right now if I had to.

What counts in my company are results. That's the bottom line, and I expect everyone on my team to follow my lead and do what needs to be done to serve our customers. If you don't do it right the first time, why would I believe that you'll do a better job the second time?

HOW TO GET RESULTS IN YOUR BUSINESS

Some people wonder what happened, and other people make shit happen.

One of my first jobs was at a car wash, when I was a fifteen-year-old in high school. The owner was a young dude himself who liked partying a lot. Working...not so much. He was happy when I approached him about a deal. The car wash was super slow, maybe fifty cars a day. I worked out a deal where I'd get ten cents a car above that daily average. He wanted to know how I would increase business, but I just said, "Not important. Just pay me ten cents a car and see what happens."

He didn't care if I ran the show as long as I handed him a stack of money at the end of the day.

When I left for college, their daily average had grown to one thousand cars.

SET GOALS

What I did back then at fifteen is what I still do in my business. I set goals and establish standardized processes. I begin with the end in mind and reverse-engineer my approach to reach that objective. At the car wash, I hired a bunch of my friends and told them: there's only one rule—put out a clean car.

They looked at me like I was crazy. *Of course, we'll put out a clean car. It's a car wash*, they were probably thinking. But I meant C-L-E-A-N. In the '80s, whitewall tires were all the rage. These tires had a white stripe or an entire white rubber side wall. They looked cool, but got scuffed up and dirty quickly, and were a pain to clean. Most car washes either didn't do a good job or charged extra. I included white walls in our standard cleaning.

STANDARDIZE PROCESSES

Next, I standardized the process. I showed everyone how I wanted the car washed in an assembly line, down to showing my guys how to brush cars with maximum impact and minimum effort, so they could keep pumping out cars. If you've brushed a thousand cars a day, you know efficiency is critical. When you have customers drive over from Detroit, you know you're doing something right. We brushed every car. We put out white walls. If anyone complained, we did it again. No questions asked.

It sounds simple, but what got the car wash from fifty to one thousand cars every day was putting out clean cars all day, every day, every car, every time. I was the de facto manager of the car wash, going to high school, doing sports, and then spending fifty to sixty hours a week at work on top of that. I never took a day off.

My business is in a different industry now, but I learned some of the most crucial business lessons decades ago, as a sophomore in high school. Setting clear goals and then building systems and processes to produce predictable, repeatable outcomes with minimal effort and maximum impact while relying on automation and standardization is what I did then, and it's what I still do now.

Customers sometimes ask me to give them preferential treatment or go out of my way, spending hours of time and effort to save them a couple hundred bucks. I don't do it. I explain that we have a system that we've vetted, processes that are best practice, and standards that we follow to provide the best bang for their buck. In business, you either standardize, or you do the running. Once you do it for one customer, it never stops. It saves a lot of hassle to cut loose those customers who don't appreciate the value we provide.

BEWARE OF HIRING YOUR FRIENDS

Hiring a bunch of other fifteen- and sixteen-year-old kids seemed like a great idea to me at the car wash. I partied with my friends at night, then showed up the next morning completely hungover and worked it off. I had learned that lesson from my stepdad. He was a prick, but when it came to work, he didn't play. You drink, and you go get your shit done. Work hard. Act like you've been here before and do what needs to be done. He didn't teach me much, but he did instill a work ethic in me that has served me well. No one could outwork me, even at a young age.

I ended up having to fire all my friends. They started expecting preferential treatment, and that wasn't how I rolled. I started hiring down-on-their-luck guys and paid them exceptionally well, so they'd show up reliably and put in their best work.

For the first time in my life, I had a real job, real responsibility, and real money. This wasn't paper route money. I bought a car. I had food to eat. I was good at what I did. I had a natural talent for business and people. I no longer depended on my mom and stepdad. I got these results on my own.

Of course, it wasn't as peachy as it sounds. I was working a car wash on 8 Mile and Van Dyke—not exactly a classy neighborhood. Customers pulled guns on the employees, people tried to rob us, and one guy screamed he would kill me after his car was damaged in the wash. In Warren, you better take it seriously when someone threatens your life. I told him what I still tell everyone. *I get off at 7:00. I'll be right outside.* I was not about to have some asshole fuck with my new sense of freedom and security.

If someone gets crazy with me, I get crazier. You really think some loudmouth punk is going to scare me after my parents tried to kill me when I was a defenseless child? Once people realized I was completely prepared to throw hands, they thought twice about threatening me.

FOCUS ON RELATIONSHIPS, NOT TRANSACTIONS

I take keeping my customers' best interests in mind at all times very seriously because I'm looking to build lifetime relationships, not to make a quick buck. I pride myself on my reputation and the reputation of my company.

When I first started out on my own, I was selling phone and internet bundles to companies. I intentionally didn't know what my commissions would be on different products because I didn't want that to cloud my recommendations to customers.

I told prospective clients that I was suggesting what I would buy myself.

Professional sales can attract some shady people, and I get why customers wonder *What's in it for that sleazy sales dude? What's the hidden agenda here?* I'll be honest, it's a little upsetting when people approach me with this attitude, but I know it's not personal. It's about them and their experience and perspective, and it has nothing to do with me. All I do is bring results all day, every day, and let my actions speak for themselves. That's why I focus on transparency and communication, honesty and integrity—and, of course, results. I underpromise and overdeliver, whether it's putting out a clean car or protecting a client from the latest cyber security threat.

I've read a gazillion sales books. Many of them talk about how to secure the best deals and give outdated advice like "whoever talks first, loses" or "whoever talks most, loses." I don't like this jostling over who gets the short end of the stick. Nobody loses in a deal with me. It must be a win-win, or what's the point in doing it? Even if I win and you lose, it's going to bite me in the ass somewhere down the line because you'll be unhappy with the arrangement. Nothing good comes from making short-sighted deals.

Results are what make my customers trust me and stick with me. For the most part. There will always be customers who are a royal pain in the ass, entitled, and unhappy, no matter what. Do not waste your time on those people. You'll end up losing money and your sanity. Instead, spend those efforts on your other customers and build long-lasting relationships based on results and trust.

FOCUS ON STRENGTHS RATHER THAN WEAKNESSES

Too often, when a team works well together or an employee outperforms everyone, we give some kudos, then turn our focus back on the challenges and problems, and the underperforming employees. That's backward in my mind. Give attention to the people doing their best, keep building them up, and encourage them to continuously improve. They'll raise the bar across the board, and employees without a growth mindset often self-select out on their own without any input from you.

RESULTS MATTER

We live in a results-based world, and my approach was always to grind it out and push, push, push. If we were having issues at NTM, I'd go beat down customers' doors, shake more hands, and kiss more babies. I could always get results by going as hard and fast as possible, so that was my only mode, 24/7. It's an exhausting and unsustainable way to live because NTM depended too much on a single person: me. And no matter how good I am as a salesperson, I'm still just one person. There is a limit, a ceiling NTM eventually hit, because there are only so many hours in the day and only so many doors I could knock on in those hours.

Leveling up with the EOS means implementing structures and processes, so I can train my team to build NTM to the point where I'm no longer needed to keep things running smoothly. I'm going back to what I learned at the car wash—standardization, automation, delegation, and setting goals.

We use EOS to create performance scorecards for all aspects of the business. In our service level agreement with our customers, we spell out exactly what we promise to deliver and then generate a scorecard report to show how we did across all these performance indicators. For example, we promise that we will resolve issues in an hour or less, and 40 percent of problems are fixed on first contact. That results in high customer satisfaction. Currently, 97 percent of clients rate our service favorably, which is excellent, but we're aiming for 99 percent.

Whenever we fall short of a promise, we discuss with our customers why we failed to meet our standard. We take full responsibility and then lay out a precise plan and timeline for how we are going to fix it. We bend over backward to over-deliver for our customers, and at the same time, we track and document everything so we can go off data rather than anecdotal statements. Recently, a customer complained to me about being on hold for thirty minutes. Once they gave me the number they called from and the day and time, I could easily follow our digital paper trail to show the customer that they were on hold for less than two minutes and that the issue had already been resolved. I never call anyone a liar, but I will push back against customers who have unreasonable expectations or simply misremember the facts of a situation.

Of course, as the founder of the company, I should not be on the phone with customers if I can avoid it. I love interacting with people, but I know I need to delegate and elevate, as EOS advises, to take the business to the next level. It's very uncom-fortable for me to step back and stop pushing so hard. I've always felt the responsibility was all mine, and now I'm learning how important it is to build out my leadership team and respect them by trusting them to do great work without micromanag-ing and interfering. This new approach takes longer because we're creating the structures and processes that will allow me to work less *in* the business and more *on* the business.

It's difficult not to chase the little wins and instead maintain my focus on building the systems that will make it possible to reel in the big wins, the transformational deals, and the exponential growth.

THINK LIKE YOUR CUSTOMER

I'm an entrepreneur and salesperson. I'm not a technical IT professional. I have surrounded myself with technical people who provide the services, but I run the business. I look at what we offer through the eyes of a consumer. Many of our competitors are run by technical people, not entrepreneurs. We have a leg up on them because I understand business backward and forward. I know how to provide excellent customer service and a seamless user experience. I know what end customers care about—because I am one.

It's like electricity. Nobody cares how it works. All we care about is that our TVs, phones, and toasters turn on when we plug them in. I understand the NTM customers who don't want to be bored with technical explanations. They just want to know that we've got them covered, that we have their backs, and that they can go to sleep at night knowing our experts are keeping them safe.

RESULTS TAKE TIME

There are no overnight successes and no magic bullets. If a company hits it big, you can bet someone was grinding behind the scenes for a decade to make it to that moment. We all love a good meteoric success story, but the reality is that people have to put in blood, sweat, and tears for years before making it big. Results in business depend on constant effort and calibration, every day, for years, sometimes decades. That story is not as sexy, but it's more realistic.

I've been working out seriously for three decades. I feel like God should let me keep this body as a reward for thirty years of dedicated service, but unfortunately that's not how it works. I had to put in the work every day for thirty years to see significant results from these daily incremental efforts. Since I quit drinking and started my personal progress and healing journey, I've seen some results, but I haven't reached that tipping point, that breakthrough, where all of a sudden, all the work I've put in reaches critical mass and triggers a significant transformation.

The same goes for NTM. Quitting drinking and the pandemic brought so many challenges and changes to business in general, the IT industry in particular, and NTM specifically. I've completely overhauled my company by being a fully present leader, implementing the EOS, and hiring new people aligned with our vision. I'm in the phase of putting in a lot of work, effort, and money, without seeing significant results yet. As you know, I'm not the most patient of people, but I try to remind myself that the results will come, and I need to stay the course.

There's no elevator to results. You gotta take the stairs.

STAY AGILE

Sometimes you'll need to experiment a lot to get the results you want. It can be frustrating to determine whether the situation calls for patience and doubling down to get results, or if you need to cut your losses and try something different. Sometimes you'll make the wrong choice, but the more you practice and learn, the better you'll be at staying agile and adapting to each situation. I can see the importance of giving the implementation of EOS a fair shot and the time it needs to produce results.

When it comes to marketing, I took a completely different route. Over the past few years, mostly during the pandemic, NTM hired several different marketing firms. The bad thing is we spent $200K on marketing strategy and tactics that produced very little or zero ROI. The good thing is that we now understand all the approaches that don't work for our business. As I've said before, sometimes the lessons are expensive, but they're still valuable. As the inventor of the electric lightbulb, Thomas Edison, said: "I have not failed. I've just found 10,000 ways that won't work."

With marketing campaigns, we have near real-time insight into conversions at every step and overall results. That helps to tweak each stage or scrap campaigns and tactics altogether. This allowed me to not get stuck bleeding even more money on marketing that simply didn't work and that was never going to work.

SHITTING ON PEOPLE IS ONE WAY TO GET RESULTS

My stepdad quit drinking after his ninth DUI, when I was about thirteen years old. I didn't think that miserable fuck could become any worse to be around, but I was wrong. As I've said many times in this book, quitting the crutch is only the beginning. My stepdad had nowhere to go with all the negative feelings and anger that surfaced that he could no longer numb and mask with alcohol. So I became his verbal punching bag. There were plenty of times I wanted to hand him a beer and beg him to start drinking again. I could take the physical abuse, but not the verbal abuse.

He was a raging, violent drunk, but sober, he was cruel and relentlessly insulted me and put me down with every word he spoke. He no longer beat me. I was getting older and bigger because I'd started working out, and he probably knew it was only a matter of time until I punched back. So he changed his approach. He often came up with home improvement projects, where he was the supervisor, and I was the worker. According to my stepdad, I was the dumbest, most worthless piece of shit he'd ever seen who failed at every task he ever gave me. I could never do anything right.

His job was making my life miserable, and as I've told you, he had an excellent work ethic.

During those early teen years, when I was trying to figure out who I was and what my place was in the world, being beat down by my stepdad every single day did a number on me. I no longer had the weekends with my dad to balance out the constant insults. Before slipping deeper into addiction, my dad would tell me I was smart, and it sustained me through all of my stepdad's insults, but now I was only hearing one side.

My internal response was blinding rage that I channeled into unrelenting determination. I would show that miserable fuck. I pushed myself harder in the gym and at my part-time job, at school and sports, always with gritty resolve and an ever-growing chip on my shoulder. You could say that the results I earned were impressive. Over the years, I got physically huge, was a respectable athlete, got into college, and made lots of money in my career.

I sometimes think that without my stepdad, I wouldn't be the hardass I am today. We often think that asshole parents, coaches, and CEOs should whip kids, athletes, and employees into shape and extract their best behavior and performance. We point to the results and say, "See! It works!" We conveniently forget that those results often come with low self-worth, doubt, anger, depression, anxiety, and even self-hate and suicidal thoughts. Those are results, too, although we usually like to ignore them.

A BETTER WAY TO GET RESULTS

Whenever I didn't get the desired results, I pushed harder, worked more, and doubled down. Now I slow down. I breathe. I take a step back. I try to stay away from extremes a little more and bring myself back to center. This practice alleviates my anxiety about the future because it creates a buffer in which I can reflect and think about what I'm going to do next, instead of jumping into action blindly.

It's uncomfortable because I've survived by grinding and pushing, so letting go of that feels scary. It felt safer to do what I've always done and get incremental results. Now I'm ready for exponential results, which requires a different approach. I'm leaning into the discomfort.

When it comes to getting results from my work family, I focus on tough love and accountability. I will have that difficult conversation with you, but I will not tear you down personally. I will expect you to do your best, but I understand we all have bad days. I will motivate and inspire you to do your best work, instead of scaring you into compliance. While the old-school way of verbal abuse and scare tactics is ingrained in many of us, it's not how I want to live my life or run my business.

I believe in collaboration rather than competition. I'm friends with most of NTM's competitors. We discuss our failures and successes; compare strategy, tactics, and numbers; and support each other. I've learned a lot from them and am happy to contribute my own lessons. There is enough work for everyone, and enough business to go around. The few people who see themselves more as competitors and don't care to share in our circle are not the founders and leaders I want around me anyway. I'm tired of the scarcity mindset. I want to surround myself with others focused on abundance. Make no mistake, this is still really hard for me. I used to make business decisions out of fear and scarcity, but I'm actively going in a different direction now and trying to let go, regardless of how cliché it sounds.

My next book might be called *Surrender*, but right now, that's still such a foreign concept. It used to sound weak to me, but I'm finally starting to realize that it means giving up the illusion of control. First, I do everything in my power to stack the deck in my favor, and then I surrender. I trust that everything will work out. I trust that everything happens *for* me, not *to* me.

The results we achieve in our personal and professional lives are all small puzzle parts to the big picture that makes up our legacy.

CHAPTER TEN

LEGACY

I'm the opposite of how I grew up. I lived that rags-to-riches success story, but my legacy won't be about material success. At first, I was all about money, cars, houses, boats, fancy dinners, and designer clothes because all I'd known was poverty and hunger. Now that I'm sober and have financial security, I realize that I want my legacy to be much more. I want to give back to society and lift up others, whether that's by sharing my story in this book or donating time and money to causes that mean a lot to me.

Every year, Ari and I adopt a family for Christmas. As NTM, we donate IT services to multiple organizations, and time to others. We look for nonprofits where ninety cents of every dollar goes toward direct services. In other words, we support the charities that run lean operations and don't pay their presidents millions of dollars in salary. A charity especially close to my heart provides prosthetic limbs to children. One of my most memorable moments was volunteering at a fashion show for these kids and accompanying a young man out on the stage.

I was nervous because the boy was nonverbal and could only communicate with his body. I was worried I wouldn't be able to figure out what he needed. I just tried to breathe and be present and really tune into him. We ended up bonding in a way that was profoundly moving for me.

I love connecting and mentoring one-on-one. Before I got my drug felonies overturned, I applied as a mentor to multiple programs, but was always rejected. I understand the reasoning behind not allowing felons to mentor people. However, a lot of people like me who've done their time, have been fully rehabilitated, and could serve as important positive role models, have a wealth of knowledge and experience to share that would be valuable to society.

When I get off kilter or too much in my feelings, ruminating about past regrets or obsessing over future anxiety, I remind myself to be present and tell myself that I'm safe and everything will be okay. As the saying goes: "So far, you've survived 100 percent of your worst days. You're doing great."

It's important to actively work toward discovering what we want our legacy to be and figuring out how to actively create it. What do you want to leave to the generations that come after you, the world as a whole, and our global community?

BECOMING THE INDUSTRY LEADER

Of course, I want to provide for my daughter and leave her a legacy of security and comfort, but I want my material and financial legacy to go well beyond my own family. Giving back to my community starts with my work family at NTM. My legacy goes further than just providing an excellent service. I want NTM to be the Ritz Carlton of IT companies. NTM is great now, but I want excellence for our team and our customers. I want my employees to be the highest paid in the industry. I want NTM to set the standard and best practices across the industry. Cybercrime is running rampant, and companies are falling victim left and right to ransomware, but not our customers.

As I'm writing this book, we seem to be heading into a recession. Inflation is at an all-time high, the marketplace is scared, prices are skyrocketing, and potential customers are trying to save a buck by making themselves vulnerable to attacks by bad actors who are getting ever more sophisticated. But NTM will stay the course. Our customers know we charge a premium because we provide top-notch service. We protect our clients and ensure they have an excellent experience every time. Their issues are resolved rapidly so that they're able to focus on their business, while we keep them safe.

I've had people tell me NTM is too expensive, turn around and go with someone cheaper, only to be crippled by ransomware, lose their customers, and be on the hook for hundreds of thousands of dollars. It's just a matter of time until businesses understand IT services are not a business area where they should go with the cheapest provider. NTM will weather the recession that will take out many of our competitors. We won't compromise our standards, which may result in fewer deals short-term, but sustainability and an excellent reputation over the long-term. Insurance companies now require businesses to adhere to strict guidelines to be eligible for cyber insurance. NTM covers all these insurance guidelines in our service agreements. We're a little ahead of the times, but pretty soon, the industry as a whole will catch up, and companies will see the value we provide.

I have my eye on my legacy as I inch toward the horizon.

DON'T TAKE IT PERSONAL

I'm convinced that my daily behavior reflects my deepest beliefs, and nothing I say matters if it's not reflected in my actions. I'm going to strive for perfection and hit excellence. Insecurity is loud, but confidence is silent. If I see someone do wrong, lie, or cheat, I understand from my own experience that it's a coping mechanism. It doesn't necessarily mean that person is bad; it means they don't know a healthier way to deal with life. I used to get angry at myself and others, but now I have more compassion. Most people are simply stuck, just like I was. They're doing their best and not intentionally fucking up their lives. I have a big heart and just want to hug them. I no longer take their behavior as a personal insult to me because I know it has nothing to do with me. *The Four Agreements* are a constant reminder that people do what they do because of personal reasons that rarely have anything to do with me. Not taking other people's behaviors or responses personally helps me focus on my own issues and the goals I want to reach to cement my legacy.

OFFERING HELP WITHOUT EXPECTATION

I deeply care about people and try to help, but if they're not ready, I move on. I see people do the same shit I used to do. They drink, use drugs, party, eat junk, don't take care of themselves, are not present for their relationships, and slack at work. They may pretend like they're living the dream on social media, but life always catches up. I see so many people deteriorating in front of my eyes. They look like shit, they feel like shit, and they act like shit. It's sad. And there's nothing I can do if they're not willing to change.

For years, my therapist told me to stop drinking and that my life would transform once I did. I loved working with that guy, but I still didn't listen to him for nearly a decade until I was ready. The same goes for everyone. If a person isn't ready to change, there's nothing I can say to convince them. Only once the pain of a certain behavior is greater than the benefit one receives will people decide to change. I can't rush that process, and neither can you. But we can be there for each other, when we're ready.

On our deathbeds, money will have no purpose. We would spend every last dollar to get more time. I've wasted enough of my life being drunk. No more. Money can't buy time, and I will use the time I have left on this earth to build my legacy. Every day you're too drunk or high or consumed with whatever other crutch you're abusing is a day wasted. Now I get to be present and do good, worthwhile things with my time. One of the reasons I often donate time over money is because I find time more valuable. I wish I had some of the time back that I wasted drinking, but that experience also made me more aware of how precious every day is. I can never get that time back, so I'll be highly selective now with how I spend my time and whom I spend it with.

TALKING TO MY YOUNGER SELF

Part of my legacy is sharing my experience with younger ver-
sions of myself. I used to be such a cocky prick, and I thought I

knew everything. I talked shit about other people being losers while I told myself I was a winner just because I had all the external trappings of success. I called other people pathetic while pissing away thousands of dollars on irrelevant bullshit to make myself feel better. I was judgmental of others because I judged myself so harshly. I had to outwork everyone because my mom and stepdad told me I was good for nothing. I chased tail because a pretty girl on my arm made me feel worthy, even though what I really longed for was a deep connection.

BREAKING GENERATIONAL PATTERNS

I'm changing the generational cycle of addiction, violence, negativity, and poverty that has affected me and so many of my family members. It stops with me. However, I don't control the generations coming after me. Author G. Michael Hopf makes a compelling point in his novel *Those Who Remain*: "Hard times create strong men. Strong men create good times. Good times create weak men. And, weak men create hard times." As the quote illustrates, it's the second generation that really benefits from negative cycles being broken, so I hope that Arianna will leverage the fact that I've turned it around before all the chaos and terror could get to her. Hopefully, her kids, if she chooses to have any, will appreciate my sacrifices and hers, and continue with the Siegel tradition. Sometimes, however, that third generation starts to forget where they came from and screws up. All I can do is my very best and hope that Arianna will follow in my footsteps.

I wish my Grandpa and Grandma Siegel, along with my dad, were here to see me now. I miss them terribly. None of them saw me quit drinking and build this new life. My dad never got to meet his granddaughter. We never had the opportunity to heal some of our family's dynamics together. I'm not a religious person, but I do believe that death is not the end. I know that wherever my dad and grandparents are right now, they are proud of me and the legacy I'm creating.

At the end of the day, I'll ask myself: How many people have I helped to get sober? How many six-figure salaried employees do I have working on my team? Is my work family happy and thriving in their personal life? What is NTM giving back to the community? What am I personally contributing to my community and the world?

COMING FULL CIRCLE

While I was working on this book, my daughter Ari turned thirteen, and we were planning her bat mitzvah. I was worried, to be honest. I wanted the celebration to be about Arianna, but I knew the large get-together would include her mom, my ex-wife, and my ex-fiancée. My sister was also going to attend with her husband and my nephew. In other words, there would be lots of opportunities for drama to take away from Ari's special day. I planned as much as I could and then let go of the outcome.

Just kidding. I didn't sleep a wink the night before. I'm not that Zen yet. My emotions were all over the place.

Ari's bat mitzvah turned out to be beautiful. It was bittersweet and overwhelming at times to see my little girl on her big day. I was able to emotionally and mentally detach from whatever my exes brought to the party, and instead focused on spending time with my daughter and our good friends. I didn't have my own bar mitzvah when I was her age; my mom and stepdad couldn't have cared less. I got to relive the childhood I wish I'd had through my daughter. I was so proud of her as she read the Torah in front of everyone and turned into a young woman right before my eyes. At the end of the night, when the pool party was in full swing, the twinkle lights were aglow, and the music was playing, she danced with her girlfriends, and all of them jumped into the pool in their fancy dresses.

I realized that the legacy I'm creating for my daughter is not dependent on what anyone else does—only on what I do. She was happy and carefree and loved that night, and I got to be the one who made it happen for her. My life is in my own hands. If $A + B = C$, it's enough to change A to get a different outcome. It's enough to only change myself to get a different result. I don't need to change others in my life. I'm free to become the person I want to be and create the life I want.

The same is true for you. Your legacy is your own.

MY WHY

Arianna is my ultimate *why* for all of the internal work I've done and continue to do. Of course, I also love giving her the material comforts I never had as a child and teenager, and take my responsibility to provide for her very seriously.

But more than anything, I want my legacy with her to be love. I have high standards and push her too hard sometimes, but I hope I also communicate to her that she is good enough and that I love her for who she is, not what she can do. My biggest wish is that she grows up to love and respect herself. I'm trying my best to lay a foundation for her to live on her own terms. I'm showing her by way of example, but instead of following my blueprint, I hope it serves as a guide for her to figure out what kind of life she wants to create for herself. I know she'll do great things because she's whip-smart, but, more importantly, she's genuinely kind.

I hope she will forgive me for the times I wasn't present, and remember the times when I was and am today. I hope she'll learn from my mistakes and knows they were my responsibility and not her fault. I hope she takes the good and expands it, just like I tried to do with my dad. All we can really hope for is that we'll do a little better with each generation, and I will do what I can until I take my last breath.

When I think about what I want my legacy to be, it comes down to being a dad to Arianna. I want her to know that although I'm flawed, I tried my very best and love her more than life itself.

WHAT'S YOUR WHY?

Figuring out the *why* behind the goals you want to achieve and the legacy you want to leave will act as a sort of stress test for your legacy. You want to have financial success? *Why?* Because you want a flashy car? *Why?* Because you want to feel important? *Why?* Because your parents ignored you? Okay, now we have something to work with. You can process your feelings and figure out if what you really want is money. I wanted to make six figures by the time I was thirty. I ended up making a lot more than that, nearly seven figures. And I still found myself asking: *why aren't I happy?*

Maybe you need therapy, a hard conversation with your parents, meditation and self-care, a practice to love yourself and silence your inner critic, to leave a toxic relationship, or quit a job that doesn't fulfill you. Whatever it is, questioning the *why* is key to uncovering how to build your legacy.

What are you going to do with your life? What do you want your legacy to be?

CONCLUSION

"No way you'll actually quit, Kelly."

When I first told a friend that I would quit drinking and change my life, she didn't believe I could do it. I tease her to this day. Hey, Allie! Tell me that it's impossible again. I'll do it twice and write a book about it. I've got receipts.

Maybe you have a supportive family and encouraging friends, and maybe you don't. But *I* believe in you.

No matter your upbringing or circumstances, anything is possible. Start by identifying the masks and crutches you're using to escape and numb your personal wounds and pain. These crutches provide temporary relief while causing long-term damage, whether it's alcohol, drugs, work, sex, gambling, or overspending. It doesn't matter.

I'm not trying to convince you to do anything you don't want to do. I wasn't forced to stop drinking. I chose to stop. I could start up again any time if I wanted to, but my life is so much better sober. No crutch ever fixes a problem—it's only a temporary escape. Now I get to truly experience life fully present, eyes wide open. Try it without your crutch and see how you like it—no need to commit to forever at this point.

Looking at yourself and your life honestly will bring you the self-awareness necessary to start transforming your life. That is the only way to process the past and move forward. Take the lessons with you, but don't allow where you came from to dictate where you're going.

You control your destiny through your daily habits, rituals, and attitude. I hope that you take away at least one thing that resonates with you and helps you live a better life. Are you willing to give an honest try and implement it into your life?

The path is different for everyone because nobody has lived your life or experienced exactly what you have. I hope you've come away from this book inspired and feeling more hopeful about the world and humanity. It really is an incredible place filled with outstanding people.

What I say and do doesn't work for everyone. But the one thing I do that I hope you steal from me is how well I steal from everyone else. I have no gurus, but I'll accept truth wherever I find it. I take a little gem from every podcast or book I come across and adapt it to my life. Nobody has all the answers, but everyone has some insight that I will search like a goldmine for what's applicable to my life and my situation. I invited you to do the same with my book in the introduction. I asked you to look for that one habit or change you would be willing to try out for ninety days.

> Now that we've come to the end of the book, what is the one thing that spoke to you most? Just start there; pick that one thing that grinds on you the most, excites you the most, or just feels right. Implement it into your life. Whether it's a daily walk, working on a creative project, or spending more quality time with your kid, commit to it for ninety days.

I promise you that the changes you'll see will have a ripple effect throughout your entire life. You'll gain momentum, and instead of being drained by adding another thing to your to-do list, you'll likely feel so energized that you'll pick a second habit to add, then a third and a fourth, and pretty soon, you'll look back on a year of progress, wondering how you got here.

When I quit drinking, I only committed for ninety days. After that, I decided, *Okay, that wasn't so bad—I'll do another ninety.* Unfortunately, that brought me right up to my favorite holiday, July Fourth. All I wanted was to kick back with an ice-cold beer and get drunk. July Fourth, 2019, was a shit day. I dragged myself out of a bad situation with a bunch of drunks who invited me to be their designated sober boat captain. I felt used and lonely and was desperately holding on to my sobriety. I spent the day alone and crying, wanting to text my ex and numb my pain with alcohol. Instead, I went home and sat in those feelings without a crutch to take the edge off. I grabbed a cigar and nonalcoholic beer and told myself that this was it. I wouldn't quit for another ninety days, but forever. The next morning, I woke up proud of myself for pulling through, like I'd conquered the next level. I had a good night's sleep. I wasn't hungover. I didn't do anything I had to regret. I stuck to the promise I'd made to myself.

Change comes incrementally. While I quit drinking on January

1, 2019, I still left the back door open, not ready to make a final commitment. Whatever change you will implement from this book, give it at least ninety days to take hold. Some may take a bit longer, some less, but you'll have a better chance of making long-lasting, transformative changes if you stick it out for at least three months.

Fast forward to July Fourth, 2022. I'm spending a day on my boat with new friends in Florida, and one of them tells me that she quit drinking after a conversation we had the previous Christmas. After six months of sobriety, she's lost thirty pounds and gained clarity over her life, and things are looking up. She winks at me, and we clink our Budweiser Zero bottles together, content in the knowledge that life is so much better like this. When we get off the boat and walk onto the beach, it's barely 2:30 p.m., and we stroll by a guy passed out at a bar, near a pile of chunky vomit smelling to high heavens, and with no friends to help him in sight. That will never be me again.

Maybe you need to get rid of your crutch, or take off that mask. Maybe you need to address your childhood trauma, or make changes to improve your health and save your life. Whatever that thing is you need to change (you absolutely know what it is, don't kid yourself), do it. Don't just sit there waiting for your birth certificate to expire.

SELF-REFLECTION, HONESTY & INTEGRITY, COMMUNICATION, FAMILY, LOYALTY, GROWTH, HEALTH, TENACITY, RESULTS, LEGACY

The values I live and work by are specifically tailored to my priorities. They may all resonate with you, and they may not. There is no one-size-fits-all way to live your life. Sharing my values with you is not meant to be advice on how you should live your life. It's an invitation to reflect on what's important to you. Do some of these values ring true? Keep them. Replace the ones that don't with others that fit better.

Money, when it's well-spent, can offer freedom and contribute to happiness. But more than money, success now means evolution to me. I feel successful when I'm learning, growing, and improving. Success means personal and professional progress, thriving to be a better father, friend, and mentor, inspiring my work family, and becoming a more effective leader and community philanthropist. The *why* that keeps me going day after day is my daughter Arianna.

What's your *why*? I'm serious about paying it forward, so if you're ready to make some profound changes in your life, hit me up.

Email me at ksiegel@trustntm.com.

Life is hard, but you're harder.

ACKNOWLEDGMENTS

Ed and Rachel Siegel for giving me unconditional love and support when I didn't know what it was.

Mindy and Harry Siegel for providing me a blueprint of what a family should be.

Ed and Lesia DesJardin for providing me a safe place to live and graduate high school.

Joanne, Leah, and Aaron, you've challenged, pushed, prodded, and loved me into the fellow I am today. Thank you.

I am especially grateful to the National Technology Management work family for your love and belief in my crazy ideas and unconventional methods. Special thanks to Chrissy, my work wife, who keeps NTM moving forward, and Sara for keeping me moving forward, always.

Thank you, Kristi, for Arianna. Without her, I'd be dead.

Aubrey, you taught me how to love.

Steve Smith, my dog, my "OG triple OG." For always, and I mean always, having my back.

Ron Karmo for always getting me into trouble, but boy, did we have fun.

Anthony Fracchia, my ride-or-die friend who took me in when no one else would. I see you, boy. You are my brother from another mother.

George and Sandy Rochette for role modeling precisely what love looks like.

Mike Roth and Darren Watts, if I hadn't met you, NTM would not exist. Thank you!

Beth Salk, you are the mother I never had. You were always there from day one, and I appreciate that.

Mark and Shanna Morin, for so many good times.

Todd, Helene, and Ian Hemmi, I love you three. You have always been family.

Lenny Berger, Dale Watts and Warren Whitehouse, the three of you set the foundation for Kelly Communications, my first company.

Thank you, Jesse Jarvis, for your unconditional love and support even when I was wrong, which was most of the time. I am proud of you too.

Chef Bobby Nahra, the baddest man on the planet. You and your family are beautiful.

Corey Silverstein, you beautiful person, you. Mr. Undefeated! Thank you for keeping me out of the legal system.

Special shout out to former WMU Deans Budd Donnelly & Diether Haenicke: challenge accepted and completed!

Tom O'Brien, Tom Gaudette, Tim Heffner, Vadim Braymin, Justin and Anton Mooter, John Bourbeau Jr., Robert Musson, Gus Gamuranes, David and Bobby Crain, Rourke Smith, Pauly Smalls, Steve Kokotovich, Brett Shadrick, Cary Siegel and kids, Kent, Judy and Mark, Brian and Kristen, Jeremiah Campbell, Ray Confer, Joey Smith, Tony Konja, Tahil Singh, Tony Avendt, Jay Feldman, you have all touched my heart in some way—thank you.

There are so many more that I forgot. I'll get you in the next book.

APPENDIX A

NTM'S CORE VALUES

APPENDIX B

1. What do you want your legacy to be?
2. What are your non-negotiables?
3. What is the first thing you do when you fail?
4. What's the most important decision you have made in your life?
5. If you were offered a mulligan in life, what would you do over?
6. What were you put on this earth to do?
7. If you were to give an eighteen-year-old one specific piece of advice, what would it be?
8. What's the smartest thing one of your teachers ever did?
9. What's the first thing you do in the morning?
10. What's the last thing you do before bed?
11. What difference did someone make in your life as a child?
12. If you were to rank all the people who have done this job in the past, tell me about number one and why you would put him/her there?

13. What do you think are the attributes that would make you a successful member of this team?
14. How do you plan to add to the strong culture that already exists here?
15. Who at your former place of work gave you the most energy and why?
16. Tell us in no more than two words what you think it is that we do?
17. What single project or task would you consider the most significant accomplishment in your career to date?
18. Tell us something that you believe in that almost nobody agrees with you on?
19. Tell us about a time when you almost gave up, how you felt about that, and what you did instead of giving up?
20. What makes you get out of bed in the morning?
21. What's your story? And, why does your story matter?
22. What reaction do people have when you walk into a room at work?
23. What are you most passionate about and how does that relate to this work opportunity?

ABOUT THE AUTHOR

KELLY SIEGEL is the CEO of National Technology Management (NTM). He has an educational background in criminal justice and sociology from Western Michigan University. Kelly has been delivering results since running his first paper route as a twelve-year-old. Besides his goal to make NTM the gold standard of the IT industry, his mission in life is to leave a legacy, or in Kelly's words, "make a dent." His relentless drive to better himself is breaking his family's cycle of abuse, addiction, and poverty. Kelly takes personal progress to the next level by continuously improving his physical, emotional, and mental health and performance by working out daily, reading voraciously, and practicing mindfulness. You'll find him feeding people at spontaneous cookouts in his backyard, volunteering his time for causes close to his heart, and mentoring the next generation of leaders. Kelly lives in Michigan with his daughter Arianna, their Yorkie Sammy, and cat Felix. He spends as much time as possible in Florida, preferably out on the water with Ari and good friends.